TO THE READER

This book is presented in its original form and is part of the religious literature and works of Scientology® Founder, L. Ron Hubbard. It is a record of Mr. Hubbard's observations and research into the nature of man and each individual's capabilities as a spiritual being, and is not a statement of claims made by the author, publisher or any Church of Scientology.

Scientology is defined as the study and handling of the spirit in relationship to itself, universes and other life. Thus, the mission of the Church of Scientology is a simple one: to help the individual regain his true nature, as a spiritual being, and thereby attain an awareness of his relationship with his fellow man and the universe. Therein lies the path to personal integrity, trust, enlightenment, and spiritual freedom itself.

Scientology and its forerunner and substudy, Dianetics, as practiced by the Church, address only the "thetan" (spirit), which is senior to the body, and its relationship to and effects on the body. While the Church is free, as all churches are, to engage in spiritual healing, its primary goal is increased spiritual awareness for all. For this reason, neither Scientology nor Dianetics is offered as, nor professes to be physical healing, nor is any claim made to that effect. The Church does not accept individuals who desire treatment of physical or mental illness but, instead, requires a competent medical examination for physical conditions, by qualified specialists, before addressing their spiritual cause.

The Hubbard® Electrometer, or E-Meter, is a religious artifact used in the Church. The E-Meter, by itself, does nothing and is only used by ministers and ministers-in-training, qualified in its use, to help parishioners locate the source of spiritual travail.

The attainment of the benefits and goals of the Scientology religion requires each individual's dedicated participation, as only through one's own efforts can they be achieved.

We hope reading this book is only one step of a personal voyage of discovery into this new and vital world religion.

THIS BOOK BELONGS TO

SCIENTOLOGY 8-8008

SCIENTOLOGY 8-8008

L. RON HUBBARD

Bridge

Publications, Inc.

A
HUBBARD®
PUBLICATION

———∞———

Published in the USA by
Bridge Publications, Inc.
4751 Fountain Avenue
Los Angeles, California 90029

ISBN 978-1-4031-4416-4

 Important Note

In reading this book, be very certain you never go past a word you do not fully understand. The only reason a person gives up a study or becomes confused or unable to learn is because he or she has gone past a word that was not understood.

The confusion or inability to grasp or learn comes AFTER a word the person did not have defined and understood. It may not only be the new and unusual words you have to look up. Some commonly used words can often be misdefined and so cause confusion.

This datum about not going past an undefined word is the most important fact in the whole subject of study. Every subject you have taken up and abandoned had its words which you failed to get defined.

Therefore, in studying this book be very, very certain you never go past a word you do not fully understand. If the material becomes confusing or you can't seem to grasp it, there will be a word just earlier that you have not understood. Don't go any further, but go back to BEFORE you got into trouble, find the misunderstood word and get it defined.

 Glossary

To aid reader comprehension, L. Ron Hubbard directed the editors to provide a glossary. This is included in the Appendix, *Editor's Glossary of Words, Terms and Phrases*. Words sometimes have several meanings. The *Editor's Glossary* only contains the definitions of words as they are used in this text. Other definitions can be found in standard language or Dianetics and Scientology dictionaries.

If you find any other words you do not know, look them up in a good dictionary.

FOREWORD

FOREWORD

8-8008:

The Attainment of Infinity (8)

by the Reduction of the Apparent Infinity (8)

of the MEST Universe to Zero (0)

and the Increase of the Apparent Zero (0)

of One's Own Universe to Infinity (8)

Originally published in November 1952, *Scientology 8-8008* was authored to serve as the textbook for students of the legendary *Philadelphia Doctorate Course,* a series of seventy-six lectures delivered by L. Ron Hubbard in December 1952 and January 1953.

Barely two months after his delivery of the Doctorate Course, Ron arrived at another major plateau. He presented this new material in another series of lectures, *The Factors,* delivered in London through March and April 1953.

To incorporate this new material and its significance into *Scientology 8-8008,* Ron authored several supplementary chapters.

Through extensive research of LRH's archives, his original manuscripts have been found and for the first time are presented to you as he intended.

- Book One of this edition contains the complete book provided the original students of the *Philadelphia Doctorate Course* and directly corresponds to those lectures.

- Book Two contains all supplementary LRH chapters and a study of these directly corresponds to *The Factors* lectures.

In summary, this edition of *Scientology 8-8008* brings together the 1952 original and the additions of 1953 for a complete view of the technology and its development. Studied in conjunction with the *Philadelphia Doctorate Course* and *Factors* lectures, this book makes possible an unprecedented level of duplication and understanding of this watershed period of Ron's research and discovery.

We are proud to present the preeminent codification of the potentials of theta — *Scientology 8-8008*.

—The Editors

Contents

Book Two
1953
Part One: The Factors

Part Two:
Standard Operating Procedure 8: Operating Thetan

$\mathscr{P}$REFACE

PREFACE

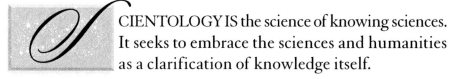

CIENTOLOGY IS the science of knowing sciences. It seeks to embrace the sciences and humanities as a clarification of knowledge itself.

One studies to know a science. His study is without avail when he does not know the science of study.

One lives and learns of life. But life is not comprehensible to him, no matter how much he lives, unless he knows the science of life itself.

One studies the humanities. If he does not know how to study the humanities, he often fails.

The physicist and the fission bomb expert know physics but not the humanities. They do not conceive the relationship and thus physics itself fails.

Into all these things—biology, physics, psychology and life itself—the skills of Scientology can bring order and simplification.

One lives better with Scientology since life, understood and controlled, becomes livable.

A civilization could fare better with Scientology since it would not be pockmarked with unknowns and rendered null with chaos.

The only richness there is, is understanding. That is all that Scientology has to give.

L. RON HUBBARD

"The thetan is immortal

and is possessed of capabilities well in

∞

Book One

1952

excess of those hitherto predicted for Man."

∞

Part One

The Beingness of Man

"At 40.0 space and beingness can be considered to be interchangeable."

Chapter One

THE
BEINGNESS
OF MAN

"The basic goal of Man, which embraces all his activities, is apparently Survival."

THE BEINGNESS OF MAN

SCIENTOLOGY IS DEFINED as the science of knowing how to know. It embraces the entire field of knowledge and includes (as part of this) the human mind, which could be considered as a computer of and vessel for knowledge.

The science has many branches (as would any proper science of knowledge) and these embrace what were designated, in the past, as the "humanities." Education, sociology, criminality, psychology and other such studies have their proper place in the framework of Scientology.

Built on organized axioms, the science more closely resembles an "exact science," such as physics or chemistry or mathematics (such as geometry), for its definitions are precise and from them proceed the resolution of problems which have been of interest to Mankind but which, until now, did not have satisfactory solution.

The essence of Scientology is its practicality.

Its application is broad and its results are uniformly predictable. It was designed to "make the able more able," not to "treat" the psychotic or neurotic or psychosomatically ill. But its application in the latter, when done by a competent and properly trained practitioner, forms the only thoroughly validated psychotherapy known to Man today and, by its use, some 70 percent of Man's ills may be remedied at a cost of time and money lower than any other similar effort and with higher effectiveness.

The science falls within the classic definition of "sciences" and is probably more vigorously organized than other groups of data which bear the designation. It is derived from closely defined axioms of Scientology which predict phenomena which are then uniformly discoverable in the real universe.

Any study of knowledge could not but be intimately connected with the beingness of Man and the earliest axioms of Scientology began to predict, and then later developments eventually discovered, the highest-level data so far obtained on the identity and capability of life.

The well-beingness and, indeed, the continued survival of Mankind depend upon an exact knowledge of his own capabilities and, this more particularly, of his relationship to knowledge itself.

Basic Goal

The basic goal of Man, which embraces all his activities, is apparently *Survival.*

Survival might be defined as an impulse to persist through time, in space, as matter and energy.

Dynamics

The impulse to Survive is found to contain eight sub-impulses. These are:

First, the urge to survive as self;

Second, the urge to survive through sex and the extension of children;

Third, the impulse to survive as a group;

Fourth, the impulse to survive as Mankind itself;

Fifth, the urge to survive as animal life;

Sixth, the impulse to survive as the material universe of matter, energy, space and time;

Seventh, the impulse to survive as a spirit; and

Eighth, the impulse to survive as what may be called the Supreme Being.

The above sub-impulses are called *dynamics.*

Combined, they form the overall urge toward Survival. But each one, of itself, plays its important role both in the individual and in the wider sphere named as a part of each impulse. Thus we see the interdependency of the individual with the family, with the group, with the species, with life forms, with the material universe itself, with spirits and with God. And we see the dependency of each of these upon the individual as a part of it.

The human mind could be conceived to be the recorder, computer and solver of problems relating to survival.

Thought

Scientology introduces new and more workable ways of thinking about things.

It has found that an *absolute* is unobtainable. Neither *zero* or *infinity* are, as themselves, discoverable in the real universe but, *as absolutes,* may be posed as symbols for an abstraction which could be supposed to exist in fact. Therefore, there would be no absolute good and no absolute evil. A thing to be "good" would depend on the viewpoint of the observer. And the same condition would exist for "bad."

An optimum solution to any problem would be that solution which brought the greatest benefits to the greatest number of dynamics. The poorest solution would be that solution which brought the fewest benefits to the least number of dynamics. And, here, a benefit would be defined as that which would enhance survival. Activities which brought minimal survival to a lesser number of dynamics and damaged the survival of a greater number of dynamics could not be considered rational activities.

While there could be no absolute right and absolute wrong, a right action would depend upon its assisting the survival of the dynamics immediately concerned, a wrong action would impede the survival of the dynamics concerned.

Thought is sub-divided into data. A datum would be anything of which one could become aware, whether the thing existed or whether he created it.

Creativeness could be found to exceed existence itself. By observation and definition, it is discoverable that thought does not necessarily have to be preceded by data, but can create data.

Imagination can, then, create without reference to pre-existing states and is not necessarily dependent upon experience or data and does not necessarily combine these for its products. Imagination could be classified as the ability to create or forecast a future or to create, change or destroy a present or past.

Cause is motivated by the future.

Statics and Kinetics

Scientology, as it applies to life, is seen as a study in *statics* and *kinetics*—which is to say, a study of the interplay between no motion and all motion, or less motion and more motion.

In thought itself, at its highest range, we discover the only true static known. In physics, a static is represented as a body at rest. But it is known in physics that a body at rest is yet an equilibrium of forces and is itself in motion, if only on the level of molecular motion. A true static would contain no motion, no time, no space and no wavelength. To this static, in Scientology, is assigned the mathematical symbol *theta* (θ). This designation means, solely, a theoretical static of distinct and precisely defined qualities with certain potentials.

The all-motion or more-motion kinetic is termed MEST. This word represents the material universe or any universe. It is combined from the first letters of the four words: *Matter, Energy, Space* and *Time.*

The interplay between theta and MEST results in activities known as *life* and causes the animation of living life forms. In the absence of an interplay, the life form is dead.

The beingness of Man, by which is meant Homo sapiens, derives its impulses toward thought and action from theta and takes its material form in MEST.

Anatomy of the Beingness of Man

Man, Homo sapiens, is a composite being of four distinct and divisible actualities. These parts are termed the *thetan,* the *memory banks,* the *genetic entity* and the *body.*

The *thetan* (which will be described later in greater detail) can exist in matter, energy, space and time, but derives its impulse from the potential of theta itself and has certain definite goals and behavior characteristics of its own.

The *standard memory banks* and the *reactive memory banks* compose the *memory banks* of Homo sapiens. These, in the analogy of an electronic computer, are the file system. The standard banks can be said to contain data of which Man is easily and analytically aware. And the reactive banks are those which contain stimulus-response experience, the action of which is below the level of his awareness. The content of the reactive banks was received during moments of lessened awareness, such as the unconsciousness of early life, in times of weariness, severe pain or heavy emotional stress, such data operating automatically thereafter to command the person without his consent. The standard memory banks are those in which experience is stored for use in the estimation of the effort necessary for survival and are concerned with analytical thought. There is an additional storage of memory itself, in a purer form than in these banks, but this memory is contained in the capabilities of the thetan.

The *genetic entity* is that beingness, not dissimilar to the thetan, which has carried forward and developed the body from its earliest moments along the evolutionary line on Earth.

CHAPTER ONE
THE BEINGNESS OF MAN

And which, through experience, necessity and natural selection, has employed the counter-efforts of the environment to fashion an organism of the type best fitted for survival, limited only by the abilities of the genetic entity. The goal of the genetic entity is Survival on a much grosser plane of materiality.

The *body,* itself, is a carbon-oxygen engine which runs at a temperature of 98.6° on a low-combustion fuel generally derived from other life forms. The body is directly monitored by the genetic entity in activities such as respiration, heartbeat and endocrine secretions, but these activities may be modified by the thetan.

The human mind could be said to be the primary activity of the *thetan,* with his own memory and ability plus the analytical standard *memory banks,* modified by the reactive memory banks of the *genetic entity* and limited by the mechanical abilities and adaptabilities in action of the *body* itself.

These four parts of Homo sapiens are detachable one from the other.

The personality and beingness which actually is the individual and is aware of being aware, and is ordinarily and normally the "person" and who the individual thinks he is, *is* the thetan. And this awareness can continue, is clarified and is not interrupted by a detachment from the body, which is accomplishable by standard processing.

The thetan is immortal and is possessed of capabilities well in excess of those hitherto predicted for Man. And the detachment accomplishes, in the sober practice of science, the realization of goals envisioned, but questionably, if ever obtained in spiritualism, mysticism and allied fields.

The anatomy of the beingness of Man is one of the lesser studies of Scientology, where that beingness relates only to Homo sapiens. For detachment of the *thetan,* by Standard Operating Procedure, is in common practice a simplicity. And it is therefore unrewarding to explore to much greater depths the remaining combination of the *standard and reactive banks,* the *genetic entity* and the *body,* since the last three are a specialized combination. Nevertheless, the development of the technology necessary to bring about a complete state of beingness, of that which Man actually is found to be, provided considerable data and technology in the field of memory recordings, the peculiarities of energy behavior around and about the body itself, as well as the construction of the real universe. The bulk of the data which concerns Homo sapiens, other than the beingness of the thetan, has been covered adequately earlier and elsewhere.

The beingness of Man is essentially the beingness of theta itself acting in the MEST and other universes in the accomplishment of the goals of theta and under the determination of a specific individual and particular personality for each being.

NOTE: In earlier efforts to better his state of beingness, Man has considered Homo sapiens as an inseparable unit which was either alive or dead. Further, Man has thought it necessary, when he thought about it at all, to address and reduce the inroads of the past before the individual could assume any high level of beingness in the present. In Dianetics, it was found that the mind was sub-divisible into two parts. The first was the *analytical mind* which did the actual thinking and computing for the individual but which, in the present civilized state of Man, was almost submerged. The second was the *reactive mind.* The reactive mind was considered to be a stimulus-response mechanism which derived and acted upon the data of experience without thought. The content of the reactive mind was found to be the accumulated bad experiences of the organism not only in its current lifetime, but in the other lifetimes which it apparently had led in order to accomplish the task of evolution and to arrive at its present state of structural beingness. The reactive mind was the blueprint. But it was also the stimulus-response dictator of action.

CHAPTER ONE
THE BEINGNESS OF MAN

The formula which described the reactive mind was that *everything is identified with everything*. Dianetics accomplished a great deal in the elevation of beingness by reducing the most violent incidents in the reactive mind by a process known as the "erasure of engrams." An *engram* was a period of momentary or long pain and unconsciousness, such as would occur in an injury, operation or illness. Such incidents could be reduced simply by "returning" the individual to the moment of the accident and then going over the accident step by step, perceptic by perceptic, as though it was happening again. After this had been done several times, the accident was found to have no more command value upon the individual. The reduction of the command value of the reactive mind was found to be necessary to a proper resolution of aberration. Understand that the reduction of the command value of the reactive mind was the goal, not merely the reduction of the reactive mind. When one is addressing the problems of an individual or group of men, the reduction of the command value of the reactive mind is still the goal where Scientology is used as a process to eradicate aberration. But two other methods are available for reducing this command value. The first of these lies in the removal of the analytical mind from proximity to the reactive mind and the increase, then, of the potential of the analytical mind until it can command and handle any reactive mind with ease. The second is simply the rehabilitation of the analytical mind by permitting it to use its creative ability in the construction of a universe of its own. It was found that there was no purpose in reducing incidents out of the reactive mind beyond the point where the analytical mind could step apart from the reactive mind and then command it. Dianetics is a therapy which addresses itself directly to the reactive mind to reduce the command value of that reactive mind. Scientology is an embracive subject, much wider in application. It has as its goal the beingness that can exist without any energy or matter—which is to say, without time—whether Homo sapiens or not. Dianetics was an evolutionary step, a tool which had use in arriving at a higher level of knowledge. Its use, however, produced slower results and much lower goals. Further, Dianetic processes were limited in that they could not be applied more than a few hundred hours without the reactive mind assuming a very high command level over the analytical mind, due to the fact that the reactive mind was being validated continually in the process, whereas the better process was to validate the analytical mind. Medicine and psychology, as practiced today, have absorbed and are using many of the principles of Dianetics without caring to be aware of the later developments in the field of the mind as represented here. Thus the society absorbs and very often misunderstands knowledge. —LRH

Chapter Two

THETA–MEST
THEORY

*"In Scientology,
the static is called
by the mathematical
symbol theta.
The kinetic is
called MEST."*

Theta–Mest Theory

CIENTOLOGY IS ESSENTIALLY a study of *statics* and *kinetics*. If anything, it is more exact than what are called the physical sciences. For it is dealing with a theoretical static and a theoretical kinetic, which are at the opposite ends of a spectrum of all motion.

One of the most valuable contributions of Scientology to knowledge is the definition of a true static:

A static has no motion; it has no width, length, breadth, depth; it is not held in suspension by an equilibrium of forces; it does not have mass; it does not contain wavelengths; it has no situation in time or space.

Formerly a static was defined only as "a motionless object," which definition is not adequate since an object or a state of rest for an object is attained only by an equilibrium of forces. And all objects have in themselves, if only on a molecular level, motion and exist in space—which is itself an integral portion of motion.

Hence, we see we are dealing with a higher-level static.

The capabilities of the static are not limited.

The static interacts with the kinetic, which is considered to be the ultimate of motion.

In Scientology, the static is called by the mathematical symbol *theta*. The kinetic is called MEST.

Theta can be the property or beingness of any individual and is, for our purposes, considered to be individualistic for each individual.

MEST stands for *Matter, Energy, Space* and *Time* and is a composite of the first letter of each. The word "MEST," appearing all by itself, denotes the physical universe. "(mest)," with a designation word after it, designates another's universe.*

The original of the Theta–MEST Theory may be found in *Science of Survival* (1951). After the concept of the true static was reached, problems of processing began to solve much more rapidly. And the main proof of the Theta–MEST Theory is its workability and the fact that it predicted an enormous amount of phenomena which, when looked for, were found to exist and which, when applied, resolved cases rapidly.

It is now considered that the origin of MEST lies with theta itself and that MEST, as we know the physical universe, is a product of theta.

The physicist has adequately demonstrated that matter seems to be composed of energy which has become condensed in certain patterns. It can also be adequately demonstrated, in Scientology, that energy seems to be produced by and to emanate from theta. Thus it could be considered that theta, producing energy, condenses the space in which the energy is contained, which then becomes matter.

---

*When we say MEST, we mean the physical universe. And when we talk about another's universe, we use parentheses with small letters (mest). Example, (mest) self. —LRH

This theory of condensation is borne out by an examination of a state of aberration of many preclears who have been found to have descended down the Tone Scale to the degree that their own space was contracted, and who were found to be surrounded by ridges, and who are thus "solid" to the degree that they are aberrated. Further, they can be found to be an "effect" in the ratio that they are so solidified. And further yet, a psychotic treats words and other symbols, including his own thoughts, as though they were objects.

∞

Chapter Three

TIME, SPACE, ENERGY AND MATTER

"Time could be considered to be a manifestation in space which is varied by objects."

$\mathscr{T}$IME, SPACE, ENERGY AND MATTER

Time

$\mathscr{I}$T IS STATED in the 1951 Axioms that time could be considered to be the single arbitrary and might thus be the single source of human aberration. A further investigation and inspection of time has demonstrated it to be the action of energy in space and it has been found that the duration of an object roughly approximates its solidity.

Time could be considered to be a manifestation in space which is varied by objects. An object could be considered to be any unit manifestation of energy, including matter.

It can be readily established that an individual loses his self-determinism in the ratio that he possesses objects and utilizes force.

Time could be considered to be an abstract term assigned to the behavior of objects. It can be found to be regulatable by postulates.

The desire, enforcements and inhibitions in the possession, giving and receiving of objects can be found to establish a time track.

Time, in the field of behavior and experience, becomes *having.*

Having and not-having form, themselves, the interchanges which become Survival.

If the auditor processes having, giving and receiving energy and items, he will discover that he is processing time directly and has processed into a higher level the time sense and reaction of the preclear.

The primary manifestation of this is found in criminality, where the individual is unable to conceive the investment of energy to attain an object. He will not "work"! The criminal in particular wishes to collapse, and render without time, *desiring* and *having.* Whereas this may be possible in one's own universe, it is not possible in the MEST universe. The MEST universe is so planned as to make *work* necessary to *have,* thus establishing a gradient scale of having. The criminal has not made the distinction between his own universe (which he possibly once had and where he could attain things instantaneously) and the MEST universe, and thus has "no respect for property." The identification of his own universe with the MEST universe is so marked as to be in itself a highly aberrated identification, thus rendering his conduct destructive to himself and causing him to fail.

Space

Space is created by a thetan. He may also conserve, alter and destroy space.

Space is the first condition necessary to action. The second condition necessary is energy. The third condition is possession or not-possession.

For the purpose of processing (and possibly for many other purposes) *space* can be considered to be the equivalent, in experience, of *beingness*. One *is* as much as he has space and as much as he can alter and occupy that space.

Energy

The qualities of energy are three in number. The first is its *existing characteristics*. The second is its *wavelength*. The third is its *direction of flow* or *absence of direction of flow*.

The characteristics can be divided into three classifications in their turn. These are *flows, dispersals* and *ridges*.

The flow is a transfer of energy from one point to another. And the energy in a flow can have any type of wave, from the simplest sine waves to the most complex noise waves. Flowingness is simply the characteristic of transferringness.

A dispersal is primarily a number of flows extending from a common center. The best example of a dispersal is an explosion. There is such a thing as an in-dispersal. This would be where the flows are all traveling toward a common center. One might call this an implosion. Outflow and inflow from a common center are classified alike, under dispersal, for handy classification.

The third type of energy characteristic is the ridge. A ridge is essentially suspended energy in space. It comes about by flows, dispersals or ridges impinging against one another with a sufficient solidity to cause an enduring state of energy. A dispersal from the right and a dispersal from the left, colliding in space with sufficient volume, create a ridge which then exists after the flow itself has ceased. The duration of ridges is quite long.

Wavelength is the relative distance from node to node in any flow of energy. In the MEST universe, wavelength is commonly measured by centimeters or meters. The larger the number, the lower the wavelength is considered to be on the gradient scale of wavelengths. The smaller the number, the higher the wavelength is considered to be on the gradient scale. Radio, sound, light and other manifestations each has its own place on the gradient scale of wavelengths. Wavelength has no bearing upon wave characteristic, but applies to the flow or potential flow. A ridge has potential flow which, when released, may be supposed to have a wavelength. The various perceptions of the body and the thetan, each one, is established by a position on the gradient scale of wavelengths. They are, each one, an energy flow.

Direction of flow, relative to the thetan, is of primary interest in energy study. There would be outflow and inflow. There could be outflow and inflow for a source-point exterior to the thetan and caused by that source-point. And there could be outflow and inflow by the thetan himself, caused by the thetan himself.

Matter

Matter is supposed to be a condensation of energy. The more energy condenses, the less space it occupies and the greater its endurance becomes. A flow of energy has a brief duration. Flows of energy meeting and causing ridges obtain greater solidity and longer duration.

The solidification of *matter* is found to be, itself, duration or *time*.

Energy becomes matter if condensed. Matter becomes energy if dispersed.

CHAPTER THREE
TIME, SPACE, ENERGY AND MATTER

The manifestations of energy are essentially, at long length, the manifestations of matter. One cannot consider matter without also considering energy.

In processing, no differentiation is made between matter and energy beyond labeling the freer-flowing and more instantaneous forms "action" and the more solid and enduring forms "having."

In order to have matter, one must have space, must have energy and must *have.*

∞

∞

AFFINITY, COMMUNICATION AND REALITY

"A very important triangle in Scientology is the Triangle called ARC."

Chapter Four

AFFINITY, COMMUNICATION AND REALITY

*I*N HUMAN EXPERIENCE (which is probably an experience senior to and creative of such things as the material universe) *space, energy* and *matter* become *beingness, doingness* and *havingness*.

Beingness is space regardless of energy and matter.

Doingness requires both space and matter.

And havingness requires space and energy.

We have a gradient scale from space to matter which starts at the arbitrary number of 40.0 for our purposes, and goes down to 0.0 for the purpose of Homo sapiens, and to –8.0 for the purpose of estimating a thetan. This gradient scale is called the *Tone Scale*.

Space is found to be a broad characteristic from top to bottom of the scale and necessary to each part of it. But it is discovered that one has less and less space the more the scale is descended. If one were to attain zero space for himself, he would attain, even as a thetan, zero.

That the body has space and the thetan apparently (to himself) does not have space is mainly responsible for the feeling of not-beingness, on the part of the thetan, which causes him to forget his own identity.

On this Tone Scale we have a theoretical point of no energy at 40.0 and a point where energy begins to be solid around 0.0. Well below this level we have matter formed of the type known as the material universe. Thus one can see that this Tone Scale is a gradient scale of energy and that the energy is free toward the top of the scale and becomes less free and more fixed as one descends the scale.

A very important triangle in Scientology is the Triangle called ARC. This means *Affinity, Reality* and *Communication*. It was used for some time before its relation to energy was discovered or understood.

Affinity is *wave characteristic* and is the range of human emotions.

Human emotions manifest themselves in energy flows, dispersals and ridges. As the emotions drop down from high on the scale to low on the scale, they are found to follow a cycle of dispersals, flows and ridges. Each dispersal has a harmonic on the scale, each flow has a harmonic and each ridge has a harmonic.

Looking up the scale from zero, one finds Death as a ridge and, in human emotion, an Apathy. Apathy reaches up some direction from Death, but at this end the harmonics are very close together.

There are two unnamed emotions immediately above Apathy. One of them, next above Apathy, is a flow. Immediately above that there is a fearlike dispersal.

The next named emotion above Apathy is Grief. Grief is a ridge and is occasioned by loss.

Immediately above Grief there is a flow.

The next level, however, is the next named emotion — the dispersal called Fear, which is a drawing away.

There is a flow immediately above this called Covert Hostility.

Above Covert Hostility is Anger, which is a solid ridge.

Between Anger at 1.5 and Antagonism at 2.0, there is a dispersal — unnamed but visible in behavior.

At 2.0 we have the flow outgoing called Antagonism.

Above this at 2.5 is an idle dispersal known as Boredom.

Above Boredom at 3.0 is a ridge called Conservatism.

At 4.0 we have another flow called Enthusiasm.

Each one of these points is a harmonic of a lower point.

The characteristic of energy (whether a flow, dispersal or ridge) expresses itself in human emotion in terms of affinity. Affinity, as here used, is a degree of emotion. Affinity is the cohesiveness of human relationships and can be acceptance or rejection of such relationships. Its equivalent in the MEST universe is the cohesion and adhesion or revulsion from matter and energy itself, as found in positive and negative currents and in forms of matter.

Communication

Communication is an *interchange* of *energy* from one beingness to another.

In the thetan and in Homo sapiens, communication is known as "perception." It is not solely "talk," which is a symbolized form of communication which sums ideas—which are themselves either a product of the Tone Scale or are above the Tone Scale, as the case may be.

Sight, of course, is at the wavelength of light.

Sound is recorded as hearing.

Tactile and smell are low-level wavelengths of the particle variety.

And all other perceptions can be found on this gradient scale of wavelengths, modified by the wave characteristic in terms of type (whether sine or more complex).

The auditor must realize that communication is essentially directed or received energy and is inhibited by the willingness or unwillingness of the preclear to take responsibility for energy or forms of energy. Where responsibility is low, perception is low.

Reality

Reality is established by *wave direction* or *lack of motion*.

As one ascends the Tone Scale from 0.0, he finds the realities are strongest at the points of flow and are weakest at the points where there are ridges on the scale. The reality of Apathy, Grief and Anger is very poor. But in the immediate vicinity of these there are more intense realities.

CHAPTER FOUR
AFFINITY, COMMUNICATION AND REALITY

Reality is established by agreement or disagreement or no opinion. Agreement is an inflow to the individual. Disagreement is an outflow from the individual. No opinion can be established by the proximity of the individual to the center of a dispersal or by a ridge.

Because of its wealth of energy and energy forms, the thetan finds himself ordinarily outdone in energy emanations by the MEST universe. Thus he is the target of an almost continuous inflow which causes him to have a consistent and continual agreement with the MEST universe. He seldom disagrees with the MEST universe. And the best processing one can do is to break this agreement and turn it into an opposite flow. For only in this wise can a preclear's ability to handle energy, and be responsible for it, be re-established.

If you ask a preclear to get the concept of "agreeing," he will find himself experiencing an inflow upon himself. Hypnotism is done by causing a subject to receive a continuous rhythmic or monotonous flow from the operator. After this flow has continued, the subject will accept any reality which the operator cares to deliver unto him. It is in this case, evidently, with the MEST universe and the solidity of the MEST universe is completely dependent upon one's acceptance of it in terms of agreement.

Reality, in essence, is agreement and disagreement. When one speaks of "reality," he speaks in terms of the MEST universe. The MEST universe, according to any computation one cares to make upon it, is found to consist of a high-level agreement amongst us. Those who disagree with the MEST universe are punished by the MEST universe. From the standpoint of the MEST universe, the greatest reality would be had by matter itself. And this seems to be its evident goal toward the thetan — to make him into solid energy.

The reality of one's own universe is poor because he is in a comatose state of agreement with the MEST universe. It is found on processing, however, that a preclear is in poor condition in direct ratio that he has accepted and agrees and complies with the MEST universe. And is in good and active condition in direct ratio to the degree he can break this flow of agreement and establish his own flows and thus create his own universe.

One's appreciation of the MEST universe is almost uniformly the energy which one, himself, places upon the MEST universe. In other words, his illusions. When he loses his hopes and dreams (his illusions), it is because he has lost his ability to emanate energy back at the MEST universe and is dependent upon the energy the MEST universe thrusts at him.

ARC

ARC thus forms a Tone Scale. This Tone Scale, at any level, finds a comparative state in affinity, in the reality and the communication abilities of the preclear. Thus by testing the preclear and discovering his chronic emotion, his chronic state of agreement or disagreement and his ability to communicate or not communicate, one establishes a level on this Tone Scale.

ARC forms a triangle which is, at once, with all three corners at a single level. Thus, if one wishes to create an increase of tone for the preclear (and one must do that to increase his self-determinism), he will find that he cannot raise the emotional state of the preclear without also addressing the reality and communication of the preclear. He cannot raise the reality of the preclear without addressing his affinity and communication problems. He cannot raise communication with the preclear without addressing his reality and affinity problems.

The worst mistake an auditor can make is to undervalue this triangle in processing.*

There are two positions for the preclear on the Tone Scale when he is still Homo sapiens. The composite known as Homo sapiens is considered to be dead at 0.0 and can rise on the Tone Scale to slightly above Tone 4.0. Thus, Homo sapiens has this as his Tone Scale range. The thetan, however, who is below the level of "awareness of self" in terms of space and energy, has a wider range. And as the thetan is basically the preclear (and the beingness and identity of the preclear, in actuality) this second range is even more important. This second range goes from –8.0 to 40.0 on the Tone Scale. The optimum position for the thetan is considered to be at 20.0, which is the point of optimum action. A Homo sapiens, as such, could not attain this level of the Tone Scale because of his physical limitations.

*A more or less complete Tone Scale can be found in *Science of Survival,* and Book One of that volume is devoted entirely to an evaluation of the Tone Scale and people. —LRH

∞

Chapter Five

IDENTITY VERSUS INDIVIDUALITY

"One's beingness
depends upon
the amount of space
which he can create
or command, not upon
his identification
or any label."

IDENTITY VERSUS INDIVIDUALITY

HE MOST COMMON confusion on the part of a preclear is between himself as an *identified object* and his *beingness.*

One's beingness depends upon the amount of space which he can create or command, not upon his identification or any label.

Identity, as we know it in the MEST universe, is much the same as identification (which is the lowest form of thought). When one is an object and is himself an *effect,* he believes his only ability to be *cause* is dependent upon his having a specific and finite identity. This is an aberration. As his beingness increases, his individuality increases and he quickly rises above the level of "necessity for identification" for himself as he is self-sufficient with his own identity.

The first question a preclear undergoing Theta Clearing asks himself is, quite often, "How will I establish my identity if I have no body?" There are many remedies for this. The worst method of having an identity is having a body. As his individuality increases and his beingness expands (these two being almost synonymous), he is less and less concerned with this problem. That he is concerned with the problem tells the auditor where he is on the Tone Scale.

One of the commonest control mechanisms which has been used on thetans is leading them to believe that when they rise in potential they will find themselves "one with the universe." This is distinctly untrue. Thetans are individuals. They do not, as they rise on the Tone Scale, merge with other individualities. They have the power of becoming anything they wish while still retaining their individuality. They are, first and foremost, themselves. There is evidently no Nirvana. It is the feeling that one will "merge" and lose his own individuality that restrains the thetan from attempting to remedy his lot. His merging with the rest of the universe would be his becoming matter. This is the ultimate in cohesiveness and the ultimate in affinity and is at the lowest point of the Tone Scale. One declines into a "brotherhood with the universe." When he goes upscale, he becomes more and more an individual capable of creating and maintaining his own universe.

In this wise (leading people to believe they had no individuality above that of MEST) the MEST universe cut out all competition.

∞

Chapter Six

BEINGNESS, DOINGNESS AND HAVINGNESS

"Doingness with energy and objects, as found in the MEST universe, is very far from the only method of producing existence."

BEINGNESS, DOINGNESS AND HAVINGNESS

Beingness

SPACE IS NOT NECESSARY to the beingness of a thetan when the thetan is above the tone level of 40.0 and can create space at will. He creates space to have specific beingness.

At 40.0 *space* and *beingness* can be considered to be interchangeable.

Beingness can exist without any energy or matter—which is to say, without time.

Doingness

Action requires space and energy manifestations. And the definition of action could be doingness directed toward havingness.

In order to accomplish *action,* a preclear must be able to handle *energy.*

Doingness with energy and objects, as found in the MEST universe, is very far from the only method of producing existence. This is a specialized form of behavior and may exist in any universe, but is very peculiar to the MEST universe.

Havingness

Time is an abstract manifestation which has no existence beyond the idea of time occasioned by objects, where an object may be either *energy* or *matter.*

Time can be defined as change in space. But where one attempts to define motion as change in space, the definition lacks usefulness since one does not define what is changing in space. There must be something there to change in space in order to have the illusion of time.

As was earlier discovered in Scientology, the single arbitrary is time. This is because time did not exist, as such, but stemmed from havingness.

When Man experiences *time,* he is experiencing *havingness* and *not-havingness.*

Time is summed up as "had," "have" and "will have." Goals in the MEST universe are summed, uniformly, under the heading of "will have." One engages in action in order to have.

This is one of the most important points of processing. The individual has made a postulate to have and has then gained something he did not want at every single point of the time track where you find him stuck.

Example: He desired to have a castle. He may have been engaging in an action, which would gain for him a castle, and was stopped and killed by an explosion which destroyed a wall before him. The explosion caught him with a postulate (what he would have) and gave him something he did not want. Struggling with the facsimile afterwards, the auditor will find that the incident began with a postulate to have and is now in a state of indecision since the explosion is unwanted.

CHAPTER SIX
BEINGNESS, DOINGNESS AND HAVINGNESS

Bluntly, any and all aberrative incidents to be discovered in a preclear are a reversal of havingness—where the preclear did not want something and had to have it, or wanted something and could not have it, or wanted something and got something else.

The entire problem of the future is a problem of goals. The entire problem of goals is the problem of possession. The entire problem of possession is the problem of time.

Time is impossible without possession of objects.

Thus is resolved one of the weightier problems of the human mind. The auditor may find it difficult to encompass this principle, since time may continue to exist for him as an entity—an unknown and hovering thing. If he will use the principle that the *past* is "had" or "did not have," that the *present* is "has" or "does not have," and that the *future* is "will have" or "will not have," and that the past, present and future are divided and established entirely by desire, enforcement and inhibition of havingness, he will find his preclear recovering swiftly.

∞

Chapter Seven

THOUGHT, EMOTION AND EFFORT

"*Ideas are invariably and inevitably senior to force and action, if those ideas stem from self-determined thought.*"

THOUGHT, EMOTION AND EFFORT

HOUGHT IS THE highest level attainable. It is of two varieties. One is Clear thought, established by will, which is from 10.0 on the Tone Scale up to well above 40.0. The other is thought established by counter-efforts, as in Homo sapiens, and governed entirely on a stimulus-response basis. The first could be said to be *self-determined thought*. The second could be called *reactive thought*.

Self-determined thought expresses itself as will and consists of the making of postulates based on evaluation and conclusions. Will does not exist in time when it is at this level. Homo sapiens' will, as Schopenhauer once remarked, is stubbornness taking the place of intellect. Willpower in Homo sapiens is most ordinarily demon circuit power. Free from the body and its ridges, which themselves contain stimulus-response thought, the thetan can change his postulates by making new evaluations and conclusions and can express his will directly. It is very difficult for a thetan inside the head, and fronted by the stimulus-response ridges of the body, to do other than obey those stimulus-response flows in agreement with the MEST universe.

Ideas are invariably and inevitably senior to force and action, if those ideas stem from self-determined thought.

Ideas born out of stimulus-response thought bear at times an almost indistinguishable similarity to self-determined ideas, but are occasioned by associative logic.

In Homo sapiens, it is quite common for a person to believe himself incapable of originality. This is because the MEST universe will brook no competition. Operating on a highly self-determined plane, originality is a simple thing to attain.

What is called willpower, then, could have two manifestations. The first would be actual self-determined thought. The second would be a result of an enforced or inhibited thought. When Homo sapiens attempts to use his willpower, he normally brings into flow the ridges around the body and is nullified by them and is pressed into aberrated behavior.

Ideas, when in the form of self-determined thought, exist above the level of 40.0 on the Tone Scale and extend down into the action band.

Ideas of the stimulus-response variety are occasioned by experience as held and contained in facsimiles and are actually dictated to Homo sapiens by circuits.

Postulate Processing is that processing which addresses the postulates, evaluations and conclusions of the preclear at the level of self-determined thought. Postulate Processing yet has some value when addressed to stimulus-response ideas. With Creative Processing, Postulate Processing is the primary and highest method of processing a thetan and it constitutes Scientology 8-8008.

Emotion, as known to Homo sapiens, extends from slightly above 4.0 down to 0.0 and depends upon the wave characteristics.

Effort is an even lower-level manifestation than emotion.

Matter would be the lower effort band.

∞

∞

Chapter Eight

$\mathscr{F}$ACSIMILES

"*A facsimile is an energy picture which can be reviewed again.*"

$\mathcal{F}$ACSIMILES

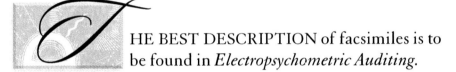 HE BEST DESCRIPTION of facsimiles is to be found in *Electropsychometric Auditing.*

A *facsimile* is an energy picture which can be reviewed again.

Facsimiles can disperse or flow when addressed by new energy, either exterior to the thetan or from the thetan. Thus the environment can set a facsimile into action or the thetan can set it into action. Homo sapiens is most normally controlled by directing energy at his facsimiles and setting them into action so as to cause him to dramatize facsimiles and training patterns.

Facsimiles are normally found to be fixed in large numbers upon ridges.

A facsimile contains more than fifty easily identified perceptions. It also contains emotion and thought.

There are many methods of processing facsimiles.

∞

Chapter Nine

Assist Processing

*"The auditor
must know
Facsimile Processing
primarily to run an
assist and in order to
know more about
the anatomy of
the human mind."*

$\mathcal{A}$SSIST PROCESSING

$\mathcal{A}$N ASSIST IS the processing given to a recently injured human being or thetan in order to relieve the stress of live energy which is holding the injury in suspension.

The direct running-out of the energy contained in the recent facsimile is done by continually running through the incident as though it were just happening (at that moment) to the preclear and recovering from it all the desire to *have* it and *not-have* it. And when this has been done to an extent where the energy is desensitized and the injury less painful, the preclear is led to handle it in different places and times and reverse it and do other things with it (as covered later, *Creative Processing*).

The assist is very important as it can cause an injury to heal or a person to recover in a fraction of the time which would otherwise be required. And in many cases it may save the life of the individual and has done so many times in the past.

The auditor must know Facsimile Processing primarily to run an assist and in order to know more about the anatomy of the human mind.

∞

Chapter Ten

CYCLE-OF-ACTION

"A life is lived in a cycle-of-action."

CYCLE-OF-ACTION

CYCLE-OF-ACTION is dependent for its magnitude upon a cycle of *havingness* because it is a cycle of *time*. But, as we have seen, *time* is an abstract term to describe *havingness*.

The beginning of a cycle depends upon a state of *havingness,* continues then in *changed-havingness* and ends with *not-havingness*. These conditions of havingness bring about an illusion of time. Where a person does not possess anything, he does not conceive himself to have any time. Thus earlier parts of the track are lost to an individual, since he has no time in them, for he has no possession in them.

The most basic description of this should be in terms of havingness, but the cycle can also be stated more abstractly in terms as follows:

Creation, Growth, Conservation, Decay and *Death,* or *Destruction*.

This would be the cycle of any object (as covered later, *Creative Processing*). It would also be the cycle-of-action as it pertains to an object in the MEST universe.

A cycle-of-action is not necessarily fixed for all universes. It is common to the MEST universe. There is no reason why, in some universe, the cycle should not run from decayed havingness into growth. But in the MEST universe, it never does (except through the point of not-havingness — death or destruction).

A cycle-of-action can also be stated in another way, this in terms of energy action. Motion is characterized by only three conditions and all motion is part of the gradient scale of these three conditions. These conditions are:

Start, Change and *Stop.*

In terms of experience, this compares to:

Beingness, Doingness and *Havingness.*

In the last 76 trillion years, the preclear has lived through "spirals." These spirals were at first very long and then shortened each time, until the present spiral for most is about forty thousand years as compared with the initial spiral of 100 million years. Thus, one can also plot the magnitude of havingness of the individual for each one of these spirals. A spiral is not unlike a life. A life is lived in a cycle-of-action. A past life is generally obscured because one does not have the body of that life (and conceives himself to now have another identity) and is not connected to the last life by a havingness. He is, however, definitely connected to his last many lives by the facsimiles of those lives which he now ignores.

Past havingness, present havingness and future havingness mark past beingness, present beingness and future beingness and also past action, present action and future action. The past, present and future are established by havingness. But havingness, doingness and beingness, alike, should be processed as intimately connected in this cycle-of-action.

CHAPTER TEN
CYCLE-OF-ACTION

The condition of the body itself and its position on the cycle-of-action, as applied to the current life, establishes to a large degree the preclear's attitude toward processing. He will react toward processing much in the manner dictated by the condition of the body and its position on the cycle. The body goes through the stages of creation, growth, conservation, decay and death. A person in his middle years desires no change and may be difficult to process for that reason, since the auditor is seeking to attain change. A person in the later cycle area will run only succumb material and will actually make an effort to succumb through processing. His incidents are commonly those of grief and loss, since these are the manifestations of havingness in decay. He has no hopes of having before him and all of his havingness, ordinarily, no longer with him from the past.

The thetan, going on the wider cycle of the spiral, is discovered early on the spiral to be in a high state of creativeness, a little later to be intent upon a growth of havingness, a little later attempting to change to avoid conserving, a little later to be conserving, and then to be intent only on decay and dying and, finally, on death itself. The auditor should differentiate very sharply between the cycle of the spiral, as applying to the thetan, and the cycle of a lifetime. He may find a very young person is still in terms of growth (and apparently the person's life should be hopeful of much living), yet the behavior of the person in general is directed almost uniformly toward succumbing.

When the thetan is exteriorized from the body, he is found to be listless and certain of the approaching end of this spiral. He is not normally aware of the fact that he will have another spiral after this or, if he is, he thinks it will be a shorter spiral—which it will be. But this can be remedied by Postulate Processing.

∞

Chapter Eleven

RELATED EXPERIENCES

"There is a
table of relationships
which the auditor
must have."

Chapter Eleven

RELATED EXPERIENCES

THERE IS a table of relationships which the auditor must have. These are divided into three general columns. Any one of the columns may be addressed first, but all three must be addressed on any subject. The vertical levels of the column can be considered to be terms which are synonymous.

40.0	20.0	0.0
Start	Change	Stop
Space	Energy	Time
Beingness	Doingness	Havingness
Positive	Current	Negative
Creation	Alteration	Destruction
Conception	Living	Death
Differentiation	Association	Identification

ARC applies to each column or for any one of the above statements of experience.

All eight dynamics apply to each column and thus to any of the above statements of experience.

∞

∞

Chapter Twelve

DIFFERENTIATION, ASSOCIATION AND IDENTIFICATION

"The widest possible differentiation exists at the moment of creation."

DIFFERENTIATION, ASSOCIATION AND IDENTIFICATION

 SPECIAL CONDITION OF *start, change* and *stop* manifests itself in the very woof and warp of the MEST universe and can be plotted on the Tone Scale.

Differentiation is at the top of the Tone Scale and is a condition of the highest level of sanity and individuality.

Association, or similarity, is the condition which exists from the upper to the very low range of the scale.

Identification is at the bottom of the scale.

The condition of the preclear can be established readily by his ability to associate. He can, however, associate much too well. Association is the essence of logic. Logic is the gradient scale of relating facts, one to another. As logic reaches the lower part of the scale, this relationship becomes finer and finer until, at last, identification is reached and thought could be expressed in terms of A=A=A=A.

(An excellent rendition of this—although one not related workably to experience and which did not have with it a truly workable therapy—is to be found in general semantics, in the book *Science and Sanity* by Alfred Korzybski.)

Insanity is the inability to associate or differentiate properly. Experience itself becomes ungoverned at the lowest depth of identity. The more fixed the identity of the person may be, the less experience of which he is capable. Fame has as its end a completely fixed identification which is timeless, but which unfortunately is matter and which equally unfortunately is inaction.

The widest possible differentiation exists at the moment of creation. At this moment one is committed to a cycle-of-action which, as it continues, is less and less governable by himself and is more and more governed by his environment. As his degree of havingness increases, he is increasingly governed by what he has had and what he has. And this determines what he will have which, of course, is less freedom, less individuality and more havingness.

Association expresses itself in the preclear in terms of the way he thinks. When he reaches the low level of association, he supposes himself to be thinking connectedly, but is actually thinking in a completely disassociated fashion—for he identifies facts with other facts which should not be identified.

The notions of a man about to die or in extreme fear are not sane. Identification brings, as its manifestation, a solidity to all things including thought. The auditor who processes a preclear very low on the Tone Scale (who is neurotic or psychotic) will readily discover that thoughts are objects to this preclear. And that time itself is a matter of enormous concern to the preclear, in many cases. Thoughts and incidents and symbols are objects.

This is commonly seen in the society in the matter of overconcern about words. A person who has sunk low enough on the Tone Scale so that words have become objects (and must be handled as such and exist without any real relationship to ideas) will stop a flow of ideas by an outrage of his word sense—which, if he is low on the Tone Scale, is easily outraged.

Differentiation, association and identification rightly belong on the scale above *(Related Experiences)* and can be processed as part of the scale above. But they are a close gauge of thought itself and of ideas. An adequate Tone Scale can be drawn for any one individual using only the above three words.

The auditor will very often find an individual who is intensely logical and quite brilliant, who is yet very difficult to process. This person has agreed with the MEST universe to such a degree that his association has assumed the proportions of near-solidity. The facsimiles and ridges of this individual have become much too solid and are, consequently, quite difficult to process. This condition of solidity may refer only to the body of the preclear (which itself is old) and it may be found that the thetan (the preclear himself) is quite vital and capable of wide differentiation, but that this differentiation is being grossly limited by the ridges and facsimiles which surround the body. Such bodies have a heavy appearance. It requires an enormously powerful thetan to handle them in spite of the solidity of the ridges surrounding the body.

Mathematics could be said to be the abstract art of symbolizing associations. Mathematics pretends to deal in equalities. But equalities, themselves, do not exist in the MEST universe and can exist only conceptually in any universe. Mathematics is a general method of bringing to the fore associations which might not be perceived readily without their use.

The human mind is a servomechanism to all mathematics. Mathematics can abstractly form, by its mechanics, coincidences and differences outside the field of experience in any universe and is enormously useful. It can best be used when considered to be a shorthand of experience and in the light that it can symbolize beyond actuality.

The essence of mathematics is differentiation, association, identification — which is to say, equalities must not be viewed as fixed in the real universe. Absolutes are unobtainable in experience, but may be symbolized by mathematics.

Chapter Thirteen

PATTERNS
OF ENERGY

*"Energy forms into
many patterns."*

Chapter Thirteen

PATTERNS OF ENERGY

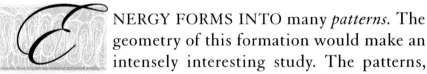

NERGY FORMS INTO many *patterns*. The geometry of this formation would make an intensely interesting study. The patterns, however, are formed by postulates and have no other existence.

The patterns of energy are viewed by the thetan in terms of *pressors, tractors, explosions, implosions, pressor ridges, tractor ridges, pressor–tractor ridges,* and *balls* and *sheets.*

The pressor is a beam, which can be put out by a thetan, which acts as a stick and with which one can thrust oneself away or thrust things away. The pressor beam can be lengthened and, in lengthening, pushes away.

A tractor beam is put out by a thetan in order to pull things toward him. The tractor beam is an energy flow which the thetan shortens. If one placed a flashlight beam upon a wall and then, by manipulating the beam, brought the wall closer to him by it, he would have the action of a tractor beam.

Tractor beams are used by a thetan to extract *perception* from a body. Pressor beams are used to direct *action.* Tractors and pressors commonly exist together, with the tractor as a loop outside the pressor. The two, together, stabilize one another.

An explosion is an outflow of energy, usually violent, but not necessarily so, from a more or less common point.

An implosion could be likened to the collapse of a field of energy, such as a sphere toward a common center point, making an inflow. It can happen with the same violence as an explosion, but does not necessarily do so.

A pressor ridge would be that ridge formed by two or more pressor beams operating against each other in conflict.

A tractor ridge would be that ridge formed by two tractor beams operating against each other in conflict.

A pressor–tractor ridge would be a combination of pressor–tractor flows in sufficient collision as to form a solidification of energy.

A ridge is a solid body of energy, caused by various flows and dispersals, which has a duration longer than the duration of the flows. Any piece of matter could be considered to be a ridge in its last stage. Ridges, however, exist in suspension around a person and are foundations upon which facsimiles are built.

Two explosions operating against each other may form a ridge.

These manifestations of energy are used in handling energy, either in processing or in action.

∞

Chapter Fourteen

BLACK
AND
WHITE

*"Black and white
are the two extremes
of manifestation
of perception..."*

$\mathscr{B}$LACK AND WHITE

$\mathscr{B}$LACK AND WHITE are the two extremes of manifestation of *perception* on the part of the preclear.

The thetan perceives best his own energy. But when he perceives energy, he desires to perceive it in white or in color. Color is a breakdown of whiteness. Seeing whiteness or color, the thetan is able to discern and differentiate between objects, actions and spatial dimensions.

Energy can also manifest itself as blackness. A space containing black energy would be black. But a black space may be only a space, existing without energy in it. This point of identification is quite aberrative and drills to permit the thetan to handle blackness are mandatory in processing. If one remembers one's fear of blackness when a child, and that evil is represented as blackness, one will see the necessity for doing this. Blackness is the unknown, for it may contain energy or it may be empty or it may be black energy.

Black energy flows are common on the Tone Scale of Wavelengths. There is, for instance, what is known as the "black band of sound."

Some thetans will not perceive anything at all because they conceive themselves to be surrounded by blackness and are not sure whether the blackness has substance or is simply empty—and they have a timidity to discover which. Such a case is resolved by making the case drill with blackness until blackness can be turned on and off and located in space and time. Although this is briefly mentioned, it is a point of the largest importance.

Black and White Running and Black and White Aesthetic Running are old processes which are not necessarily vital today to processing. However, white energy runs easily. And where the preclear has a black spot of energy somewhere on an organ or somewhere in the environment of the body, the auditor asks him to turn it white in order to let it flow away. It may not flow away if it is black, either because it does not belong to the preclear (in which case he would see it as black) or because it is simply a spot of space with which he is not familiar. By turning it white, he is able to handle it—for he now knows it to be filled with his own energy.

One can run "own-determinism," "other-determinism" as concepts. In this case, the preclear runs the one as long as he gets an area white. And then he runs the other to continue its whiteness. In such a way, all the energy in the area is drained away.

The most common manifestation of a ridge is to have one side of a ridge white and the other side black. This is because the preclear conceives one side of it to have his own energy on it and to have on the other side of it energy belonging to another. By running the concept that it is his own and then running the concept that it is another's, one runs both sides of a ridge (if he is running ridges).

Although live energy is generally conceived to be white, it can also be black. In running a preclear with an E-Meter, it will be discovered as long as a flow is white and as long as a flow is running that the needle will gradually rise. When a point of blackness appears in the field, the needle will halt and either will not rise again or will flick and give the preclear a somatic. This flick is characteristic of the somatic. The stuck needle is characteristic of the black field. The auditor can sit watching a needle and will be able to tell the preclear whenever the preclear has had a black area appear in the field. It is notable that somatics only occur in the presence of a black patch. This means that the unknown characteristics of the blackness are something the preclear has been holding away from him so as not to have or that black wave energy is that energy used to impress pain. The latter is the more probable case, although a great deal of work must be done upon this to establish beyond doubt the manifestations of blackness.

A preclear who cannot see color in his facsimiles, cannot see it because he is unable to use energy with which to perceive. He will see things in terms of blackness or whiteness. He may be able to get black or white or may be able to get only blackness. In the latter case, he finds blackness in some way profitable and desirable. And running the concept of havingness ("will have" and "have had" blackness) and using drills in handling blackness (moving it from space to space in the environment and moving it into yesterday and tomorrow—as covered later, *Creative Processing*) will bring about control on the part of the preclear of blackness.

∞

∞

Chapter Fifteen

$\mathscr{P}$ERCEPTION

"The rehabilitation of perception is essentially the rehabilitation of force."

PERCEPTION

THE ENTIRE SUBJECT of *perception* is the subject of *energy*.

As the preclear goes down the Tone Scale, he is less and less capable of differentiation and is thus less and less capable of handling energy and is more and more subject to energy, until at last he will not emanate or handle energy. Even in the higher ranges of this condition, his perception begins to diminish.

The rehabilitation of perception is essentially the rehabilitation of force. Force is rehabilitated by rehabilitating the control of energy. This is done by ARC Processing and in many other ways. The chief way in which this is done is by establishing the preclear's ability, by Creative Processing, to handle blackness.

An entire science called "perceptics" can easily be constructed and is mentioned in the Original Thesis (1948).

The rehabilitation of sight in the blind, hearing in the deaf, the ability to speak, anesthesia of the body or body areas or the genital organs, depends upon the rehabilitation of the preclear's ability to handle energy. Creative Processing, with particular attention to handling blackness, is essential in this process.

∞

Chapter Sixteen

ORCE

"Effort is defined as directed force."

$\mathcal{F}$ORCE

 N THE AXIOMS, force is defined as random effort. Effort is defined as directed force. Force is essentially measured effort.

It is quite common for individuals to be so protesting of what the MEST universe is doing that they abandon any and all force. And, if asked to re-assume force or use it, suppose that one is asking them to condone and assume punishment and destruction, since these in the MEST universe are done with heavy quantities of force.

Force, however, would be a gradient scale and could actually be called an energy manifestation, for even matter contains force.

For the purpose of processing, in order to keep from upsetting the preclear who usually has very bad connotations with the word "force," the auditor stresses instead the "handling of energy."

The use of energy would encompass any activity having to do with energy or matter.

∞

Chapter Seventeen

RESPONSIBILITY

"The rehabilitation of the thetan in the handling of energy brings about a rise in responsibility itself."

RESPONSIBILITY

THE RESPONSIBILITY LEVEL of the preclear depends upon his *willingness* or *unwillingness* to handle *energy*. That preclear who is protesting against energy in any direction is abandoning responsibility in greater or lesser degree.

One obtains randomity (see Axioms) by abandoning responsibility in some sphere. He will then find himself in conflict in that sphere.

The gradient scale of responsibility is as follows:

At 40.0 responsibility manifests itself as will and can be so pervasive that there is no randomity. This would be Full Responsibility.

At 20.0 responsibility would manifest itself in terms of action, where roughly half one's environment or space had been selected for randomity and for which one would take no responsibility. At 20.0 responsibility would be 50 percent of the total energy existing.

At 4.0 we find Homo sapiens, in his narrow environment, disagreeing (by using the emotion of Enthusiasm) with an existing state of affairs and directing energy toward the righting of that state of affairs. Even so, responsibility is low at this level.

At 2.0 blame enters the Tone Scale as a major factor. This is the level of the Tone Scale where fault is envisioned for the first time. Above this level there is sufficient breadth of understanding to see that interdependencies and randomities can exist without fault and blame. At 2.0, with the emotion of Antagonism, an individual is assigning blame for lack of responsibility rather than trying to enforce responsibility.

At 1.5 blaming is almost the sole activity of the individual and while taking no real responsibility himself, yet blames all on his environment and does so with violence.

At 1.1 one pretends to take some responsibility in order to demonstrate that others are at fault, but one has no real responsibility.

At 0.9 or around the level of Fear, one does not think in terms of responsibility, but is willing to accept all blame in an effort to escape all punishment.

At 0.5 Grief, the individual blames himself and accepts the fault for what has occurred.

At 0.05 Apathy, there is no question of either blame or responsibility. At this level one has become MEST.

On the Chart of Human Evaluation, in *Science of Survival,* one will find what might be expected to happen to material and communication and persons in the vicinity of those below 2.0 on the Tone Scale. This stems normally from responsibility or, rather, its lack.

The keynote of responsibility is the willingness to handle energy. The rehabilitation of the thetan in the handling of energy brings about a rise in responsibility itself. If a person low on the Tone Scale still exhibits responsibility, then his energy activity initially must be enormous for any segment of responsibility to exist low on the scale.

The processing of responsibility is one of the most vital processes. If one processes responsibility itself, he can expect sooner or later a Theta Clear. He would process it by "brackets."

There is a condition known as the "glee of insanity." This is essentially a specialized case of *ir*responsibility. A thetan, who cannot be killed and yet can be punished, has only one answer to those punishing him. And that is to demonstrate to them that he is no longer capable of force or action and is no longer responsible. He therefore states that he is insane and acts insane and demonstrates that he cannot possibly harm them, as he lacks any further rationality. This is the root and basis of insanity. Insanity is the only escape possible, besides death.

Death has the value of convincing others that one can no longer be punished or feel. As long as one has a body, which can die, there is a limit to the amount he can be hurt. When there is no body and there is no limit to the amount he can be hurt, his only answer is this plea of complete irresponsibility which is the glee of insanity. This is found as an actual energy manifestation in the vicinity of sanitaria and can be felt as an emanation from the insane.

If the preclear is unable to conceive "being happy about being insane" (which he usually cannot), get him to get the feeling of "anticipation for a vacation." This is irresponsibility in one sense and, in actuality, when deepened becomes the glee of insanity.

Happiness is the overcoming of not insurmountable obstacles toward the known goal of havingness. Stepping away from this track, feeling that one's work is too hard, are forsakings of responsibility. A common method employed by low-toned people to reduce the power and ability of an individual, and so place him under control, is to convince him that he is tired and overworked. If they can so convince him, they can then get him to take a vacation. An examination of an individual who has been subjected to this process will discover that he was happiest when he was working and that before he "needed a vacation," many people worked on him to convince him that he should not work so hard — and thus turned what was play, to him, into actual work. Society almost demands that a man consider whatever he is doing as work and demands that a man consider work as an unhappy thing. In looking around the society of those who gain easily, one finds only people who take a great deal of joy in working and who never think in terms of a vacation.

To run the bracket on responsibility, one would run the "desire (on the part of the preclear) to be responsible," his "desire not to be responsible," times when he has been "forced to be responsible," times when he has been "forced not to be responsible," times when he has been "restrained from being responsible," times when he has been "restrained from being not responsible," times when he has been "sympathized with because of his responsibilities." And then, all this as a bracket — the preclear doing it to others and others doing it to the preclear and others doing it to others. This, run as a bracket, and run round and round as a bracket, produces marked results.

The "joy of responsibility" and the "joy of irresponsibility" should also be run in terms of brackets.

This becomes most effective when run in terms of "responsibilities of having," the "irresponsibilities of having," the "responsibilities" and "irresponsibilities" of "having had" and of "will have."

Before this has been run very long on some individuals, the glee of insanity will manifest itself and it must be very thoroughly run out. It is often a hectic, uncontrolled laughter. This should not be confused with line-charge laughter, to which it is a cousin. A preclear who starts laughing over the serious things of his past is breaking locks and he can be made to laugh in this fashion for many hours if the chain reaction is started. The laughter which accompanies the glee of insanity has no mirth in it whatever.

Peculiar to this is what might be called the attitude of MEST. MEST is not responsible for anything. That preclear who has as his goal "complete irresponsibility," has also as his goal "being complete MEST."

MEST has no space of its own. It causes no action except when acted upon. And it owns nothing, but is itself owned.

Slaves are made by giving them freedom *from* responsibility.

The thetan high on the scale can make space or own space, has wide choices of action and can create, change or destroy anything he wishes.

∞

Chapter Eighteen

The Chart
of Attitudes

"...the auditor
should know very well
his Chart of Attitudes
and the reasons
underlying each."

Chapter Eighteen

$\mathscr{T}$HE CHART OF ATTITUDES

N ORDER TO DO Rising Scale Processing (as covered later, *Postulate Processing*), the auditor should know very well his Chart of Attitudes and the reasons underlying each.

1) Survives Dead	2) Right Wrong	3) Fully Responsible No Responsibility	4) Owns All Owns Nothing
5) Everyone Nobody	6) Always Never	7) Motion Source Stopped	8) Truth Hallucination
9) Faith Distrust	10) I Know I Know Not	11) Cause Full Effect	12) I Am I Am Not
Win Lose	Start Stop	Differences Identification	Being Had

This chart on the upper line in each of the above represents from 27.0 to 40.0. The lower line under each one represents 0.0.

Each one of these is a gradient scale with many intermediate points. In Rising Scale running, one seeks the attitude of the preclear nearest to the lowest end of this scale and asks him to do a "rising scale" in order to see how high he can change his postulate toward the upper end of the scale.

The last lines are of course a repeat, without the intermediate positions of the earlier interdependencies of experience.

Survival

One of the first principles in the MEST universe, and that principle which when discovered resolved the problems of the mind, is the lowest common denominator of all MEST universe existence: The goal of life in the MEST universe is Survival and *only* Survival.

Survival equates behavior in Homo sapiens or in any life form. It also covers the wide field of ethics. The principle of Survival was never intended to embrace theta itself. For theta has, of course, immortality and does not even necessarily move in MEST time.

Survival is nothing if not dependent upon possession, action and beingness. It is most ordinarily viewed as the attempt in a life form to persist in a state of existence as long as possible.

Right–Wrong

Rightness is conceived to be survival. Any action which assists survival along the maximal number of dynamics is considered to be a right action. Any action which is destructive along the maximal number of dynamics is considered to be wrong. Theoretically, How right can you be? Immortal! How wrong can you be? Dead!

After a certain point on the Tone Scale is reached by the preclear, he will tend instinctively to seek out and do right actions. But ordinarily Homo sapiens is thoroughly engrossed in being wrong. Social politeness, with its violation of the Code of Honor (see later text), is quite non-survival. It might also be said, How wrong can you be? Human!

The accident-prone, and the no-responsibility case in general, is so intent on being wrong that he is incapable of conceiving right.

All jurisprudence is built upon the principle that "sanity is the ability to differentiate right from wrong." Jurisprudence does not, however, give a definition of either rightness or wrongness. Thus for the first time, with this principle, rules of evidence and other matters in law can be established with some accuracy.

Absolute rightness, like absolute wrongness, is unobtainable.

Rightness and wrongness are, alike, relative states.

Responsibility

(See earlier text.)

Ownership

In view of the fact that time can be conceived to be havingness and in view of the fact that time itself is one of the most puzzling concepts which Homo sapiens has ever sought to master, the whole question of ownership is subject to grave error—particularly on the part of Homo sapiens.

Discussions in the earlier text demonstrate that individuality depends upon high tone level and freedom. And identity, as such, would be at a complete level of reduction, a condition analogous to MEST.

It has long been recognized that "A rich man may as well try to get into Heaven, as a camel through the eye of a needle." The auditor will suddenly discover this truth when he tries to process many rich and successful men. These have carried ownership to such an extent that they are themselves thoroughly encased in energy, which is solidifying into MEST itself. Instead of having things, they themselves are had by things. Their freedom in motion is enormously reduced, although they have tricked themselves into believing that possessions will increase freedom.

The auditor will find his preclear upset nowhere on the Tone Scale as he will on the subject of ownership. A childhood, for instance, is intensely upset by the subject of ownership, since the child is given to understand that he owns certain things and is then commanded in every action he takes with those items. A child cannot have possession, free and clear, of anything in the average family. He is given shoes and is told to take care of them, and is punished if he does not take care of them, although he apparently owns them. He is given toys and is harassed whenever he abuses them. He finally becomes convinced that he owns nothing and yet he is in a state of anxiety about owning things. Therefore, he will try to possess many things and will completely overestimate or underestimate the value of what he has. The auditing of childhood ownership is a fruitful field for the auditor.

That preclear who is upset on the subject of time, even faintly, is and has been enormously upset on the subject of ownership, since havingness and its manifestations are themselves the MEST universe trick of giving us an illusion of time.

Everyone–Nobody
(See earlier material on Identity versus Individuality.)

It may be confusing to the preclear that being everybody can be conceived at both ends of the Tone Scale.

The difference is that at the bottom end of the scale the preclear is making the mistake of considering the "somebodies" around him as MEST. He can be their MEST identities. At the top of the scale, while still retaining his own identity, he can be anyone's identity. But this is on a theta level and is disassociated from MEST.

That preclear who goes around believing he is other people is usually at the bottom end of the Tone Scale and has confused his own body with the bodies he sees because he does not have a proper view of his own body and so can easily mistake it for the bodies of others.

When an individual is low on the Tone Scale, he easily does a life continuum for others because he himself is so encased in MEST and so poorly recognizes his own identity that he can conceive himself to be anyone without knowing what he has done.

The question of valences and life continuums is difficult to resolve in direct ratio that the preclear conceives himself to be MEST.

MEST, lacking the ability to create and to produce directive action, is of course nobody. When a man is convinced he is nobody, he has been convinced at the same time that he is MEST.

Always–Never

We have already seen that objects give us the illusion of time. The ability to create objects is interchangeable with the ability to have an actual forever.

There would be an illusory forever, which would be dependent upon the duration of an object and its apparent solidity. One might also say that the MEST universe seeks to own one by pretending that immortality is something difficult to attain and is only purchased by achieving an identity or being an object. The ultimate in this is, of course, being a part of the MEST universe. One might say, jocularly, that every planet in the MEST universe was once one or more people.

A considerable reaction can be got from a preclear by making him conceive a feeling of devotion toward the "older gods" who were here and who built this universe and who have left it to him. Deeply religious feelings are very often based upon this idea. Some astonishing reactions can occur in a preclear when running this concept.

The real way to be assured of a great deal of time is to be able to create time. And this would be, to a thetan, the true concept of Always.

Time is created, at least in this universe, by creating energy and objects and by being able to make the universe agree with oneself — not by having the universe continually making one agree with it.

Motion Source–Stopped

The ability to cause motion is dependent, whether the individual realizes it or not, upon the ability to conceive space. Creation of space is the first requisite for the creation of motion.

When one can no longer create space and cannot conceive any space to be his own, he can be considered to be stopped. That individual who is tremendously concerned with being stopped is losing his ability to create space. When he is no longer able to create space, he is himself MEST.

Somebody once said that "It was a poor man who was not king in some corner." One might add to this that "One is not only poor, but he does not exist when he cannot create a corner." One could obtain a very amusing viewpoint of this by watching the conduct of a dog who, theta-motivated like every life form, is bravest in his own front yard. Even a mastiff proceeds with some caution when in the front yard of a Pekingese.

This is a case of ownership of space and, in some slight degree, the ability to create space to own.

One processes this by moving mock-ups into an outer created space (as covered later, *Creative Processing*).

Truth—Hallucination

The highest one can attain to Truth is to attain to his own illusions.

The lowest one can descend from truth is a complete acceptance of MEST universe reality, for this below a certain level becomes scrambled and brings on the condition known as hallucination. Hallucination is not self-generated. It must come about only when a person is an effect to such an extent that he is almost dead.

What is commonly believed to be truth is "agreement upon natural law." This would be truth of the MEST universe, which would be the lowest common denominator of agreement on any subject. Where the MEST universe is concerned, acceptance of such truths is dangerous.

In Scientology, one is studying the lowest common denominators of agreement which bring about an acceptance of the MEST universe and prohibit the creation of one's own universe, which latter ability alone makes possible perception of the MEST universe—which is, itself, an agreed-upon illusion.

Truth, in Scientology, is the study of the lowest common denominator of agreement plus the establishment of the true ability of the thetan. The true ability of the thetan is a truth much higher than the truth of the MEST universe itself. And if it has never before been known, the difficulties of communicating it have been such as to inhibit its promulgation.

It can be seen there is a truth above what passes for "truth" in the MEST universe. Scientific truths, gained from deduction and observations of behavior of the MEST universe, are themselves manifestations of agreement on the part of thetans who are capable of much wider creation and agreement than that represented in the MEST universe.

We have answered, in Scientology, a good portion of "What is truth?"

Faith–Distrust

There is no more underrated quality in existence than Faith.

The subject who, under the hands of a hypnotist operator, conceives an enormous agreement with the hypnotist is experiencing "faith" as it is commonly understood. In this state, the subject can perceive anything which the hypnotist may direct.

In order to understand Faith, one must be able to differentiate between Faith-In and Faith. The difference between these two conditions is a direction of flow, which earlier we found to be reality itself.

Faith-In is an inflow of agreement and the placing of one's beingness and doingness under the control of another and is, in other words, the sacrifice of one's universe. This is the basic mechanism wherein, all along the whole track, thetans have been recruited in some cause or mystery and have surrendered to this their own identity and ability. A little of this goes a very long distance. It is, in essence, the basic trick of hypnotism. And by it, one can concert and reduce the abilities of a subject for any purpose. Faith-In would be an inflow and would bring about acceptance of reality other than one's own.

Faith itself would be without flow, where one was in a full state of beingness. And with this condition, one could occasion Faith itself to occur within his own universe or could occasion people to have faith in him.

The auditor will find one of the more aberrative phases of the preclear as his failure to obtain, from others, faith in himself. And, his acquiescence to their demands, on any dynamic, that he have faith in them. Because it is entirely true that a being is low in tone without actual Faith, the fact can be traded upon with great ease.

Distrust is not the lowest end of the scale, but begins to set in as a neurotic or psychotic condition at about 1.5. Actually, Faith interchanges with Distrust in gradient scale levels all the way down the Tone Scale and they alternate one with the other as one goes deeper and deeper into the MEST universe. The lowest level of this scale is not Distrust, but complete Faith-In—which is the condition held by MEST, which is supine to any sculptor.

This column of Faith–Distrust might also be called the column of Belief–Disbelief or the column of Reality–Unreality.

The auditor can expect the preclear, as he rises up the Tone Scale, to pass through the various shades of Distrust and the various shades of Faith. This is often quite upsetting to the preclear, for he cannot conceive himself to be rising in tone.

It is very noteworthy that a preclear, when low in tone at the beginning, will pass inevitably through various strata of revulsion for the MEST universe and then for his own universe. The revulsion he can conceive for the MEST universe, objects, and for being in the MEST universe can become unthinkably distressing to him.

When this condition has occurred, the auditor can be reassured by the fact that the preclear is rising in scale, but has hit upon one of the levels of this column, and that a higher level and a more comfortable one immediately succeeds as processing is continued. This is simply a problem of reversing directions of flow. If the auditor is running flows, he will find that an inflow is shortly succeeded by an outflow and this outflow is shortly succeeded by another inflow. These are, in essence, agreements and disagreements alternating one after the other and each one is slightly higher on the Tone Scale than the last.

I Know—I Know Not

Epistemology has long been the senior study of philosophy. Scientology is, itself, the science of knowing how to know.

The study of knowledge is, in essence, in the MEST universe, a study of data. Data in the MEST universe is usually recorded in facsimiles. Thus, one can go in two directions toward knowledge. The first is knowing what one *is*. And the second is knowing what has happened to one in the MEST universe and searching for identity in the MEST universe.

There is no more tragic track than the sordid ransacking of facsimiles to discover truth. For all one discovers is what is true for the MEST universe. This wandering and endless trail is black with the bones of lost beingness. Earlier explorers have, almost without exception, destroyed themselves in this search for truth in the MEST universe. For all they discovered were further and further agreement and more and more facsimiles. And all they achieved as individuals were the traps and snake pits of implants on the whole track. To stand at last near the heights of discovered beingness, has withered the sadness of standing on other men's bitter and, until now, probably unrewarded search.

It was necessary to ransack the facsimiles, which are themselves one's sole inheritance for travail in the MEST universe, to discover the common denominator of facsimiles. And to discover that they were *only* facsimiles, how they were created and how experience was impressed upon the individual. One might well have the feeling of having narrowly escaped a terrible tragedy when he views the thinness on which he stood to view this brink of oblivion. For it was obviously never intended that anyone should recover from participation, or even spectatorship, in or of the game called MEST universe. Dante's inscription above the portals of Hell might very well be written best on the gates of entrance into this universe: "Abandon all hope, ye who enter here."

The common denominator of all difficulty an individual has in the MEST universe may be summed under the heading "facsimiles." Originally, in his own universe, he used the mechanism of energy creation to make objects. In the MEST universe, this ability reduces to the use of energy solely for the recording of data about the MEST universe so that one can "agree" with that data. And in this process lies death not only as a body, periodically, but as a thetan.

What has commonly been mistaken for "knowledge" has been the MEST universe track of "seeking agreement with the MEST universe," by discovering all possible data about what one should do in order to agree with the MEST universe. The more data one achieved, the more facsimiles he had. The more facsimiles he had, the more MEST he was. It was necessary to win through this trap in order to recognize, isolate and evaluate the common denominators of facsimiles and to discover that self-created energy has been utilized to enforce agreement upon oneself, so as to enslave one's beingness and lead it to its final destruction.

No adventure in the MEST universe can exceed the adventure of making orderly anatomy from the chaos of commingled matter, energy and space which comprise the planets, galaxies and island universe of this black beyond which waited to devour the universe self-constructed of any thetan or group of thetans. The slaying of a roaring beast of fire held in it, in olden times, less action and danger.

These lines are not written from any self-congratulatory motive, for fame is a rock. But by these lines, the auditor may be impressed by the actuality of what he handles so that he can appreciate his own gallantry in fronting an adversary of such insentient brutality.

The road to knowledge led through the anatomy of the space and energy masses called MEST universe. The data did not lie *in* the MEST universe. The ransacking of facsimiles for data about one's identity, about one's "past history" in the MEST universe, should be tolerated by the auditor only insofar as it gives him materials for Creative Processing. He should never directly begin the direct processing of facsimiles, whether engrams or secondaries, save only in the case of an assist. He needs only to know so much of a preclear's beingness on the whole track, to know what to mock-up for the preclear's running.

The difficulty the preclear is having is not so much the content of various facsimiles but, on this high echelon of Scientology on which we are now operating, the fact that he *has* facsimiles. The path of better techniques is the path toward permitting the preclear to step away from all his facsimiles.

The track to knowledge, then, has two directions. It is possible at this time to take the better path. The essence of true knowledge is the essence of existing so that one can create beingness and data to know. All other data is junior to this.

A control operation of some magnitude was once perpetrated in the late eighteenth century. It was stated, with great authority, that "anything worth knowing would always be beyond the bounds of human experience." This sought, knowingly or unknowingly, to further block the search for beingness. It should never be considered by anyone, or under any circumstances, that anything which can effect him could be beyond his ability to understand, or know the full nature of what he is experiencing.

If any lesson is contained in Scientology, it is the lesson that the gates to all knowledge are open. One should have the knowledge of the composition of the MEST universe as a fox might have use for the knowledge of a trap. It is cruelty to make a Theta Clear without at the same time educating him so as to permit him to avoid those pitfalls which brought him where he is found—in a MEST universe, in a MEST body, on a planet named Earth (Solar System, Galaxy 13, MEST universe).

Top-scale Knowing would be top-scale ability to create beingness. The identity assigned to one by others and the data contained in facsimiles are knowingness not worth having.

Cause–Full Effect

Above the level of all else on the Chart of Attitudes is Cause. Causation is the highest attainment which can be envisioned by the thetan. But this is not the highest possible attainment and much higher levels may be envisioned by the thetan when he has attained high on the level of Causation.

To be full Cause, one would have to be able to cause space and many other manifestations. Everyone, to a greater or lesser degree, attempts to be Cause until he is at last Full Effect. The fullest effect in this universe is to be MEST itself.

One of the principles of causation is outlined in the cycle-of-action. But it is not necessarily true that one can only cause a cycle of this pattern or that one must cause cycles at all. For it is excellent processing to mock-up with reverse cycles, going from death back to creation, with objects which one has mocked-up.

It is one of the "facts" of objects that space and energy must have been caused before the object could exist in the MEST universe. Thus any object has prior cause. For this reason, when anyone in the MEST universe begins to study in order to resolve some of the riddles of the MEST universe, he falls into the trap of supposing all cause to be prior and time itself to exist. This would make one the later effect of everything he caused. In other words, if he made a postulate, he would then immediately afterwards become the effect of that postulate. Cause—motivated by "future" desire, enforcement and inhibition of havingness—does not lie in the past, but only in the condition of havingness in this universe which states that any object must have had a "prior" cause.

The preclear has become aberrated by the process of making an effect out of him and taking from him the ability to be cause by convincing him that it is better to be an effect.

Freud had one of the major aberrations in view when he declared his libido theory (in 1894) and declared therein that sex was the only aberration. It is certainly a major one in Homo sapiens, for in sex one desires to be the cause of little or nothing and desires to be the effect of pleasurable sensation.

Anything in the MEST universe which one desires, he desires because it will have a pleasant effect on him. Thus he is searching for sensation caused exterior to himself which will make of him an effect. How much of an effect can he become? MEST!

The snare of pleasurable sensation leads one to accept energy other than one's own. Desire for this energy, or objects, then puts one in the condition of being an effect. When one is surrounded by as many powerful possible energy sources as one finds in the MEST universe, he cannot but become a low-level cause.

When a preclear is at a level on the Tone Scale (above 8.0) where he is concerned with "bad" and "good" (both these are seen broadly enough to understand that they are viewpoints), he is very concerned if he thinks that he is or could be bad cause and is desirous of being what he considers good cause. He judges these things by moral codes and so bends his conduct as to make bad cause antipathetic to himself and others. Thus he gives away responsibility for bad cause and, in that very action, becomes the effect of bad cause. When he has found himself to be what he considers bad cause, he ceases to "trust" himself and begins to blame himself and then others. All angels have two faces. They are commonly represented in mythology as having a black and a white face. To be complete Cause, theoretically, a person would have to be willing to be bad cause and good cause. Only in this way, in the MEST universe, could he escape the liability of becoming the effect of bad cause.

The criminal who has elected himself bad cause, through having found it impossible to trust himself, can only escape becoming an effect by fighting all good cause. And a criminal career always begins at the moment when the criminal-to-be loses his self-respect. A career of prostitution cannot begin until self-respect is lost. And self-respect is only lost when one considers himself to be bad cause. The reformation or reclamation of the criminal does not depend upon punishment, which only seeks to make him more MEST than he is, nor yet upon good cause which he must fight, but upon the re-establishment of the criminal's self-respect. For only after this is he capable of being good cause.

An entire process evolves around:

"What would you cause on each one of the dynamics?"

An assessment of the preclear, with a meter, should seek to establish where the preclear feels he would be bad cause. For it is on this point that he will be found to have lost his self-respect and where it will be discovered why he cannot trust himself.

Self-trust, self-respect and the ability to be Cause are conditions in the same order of magnitude and can be interchangeably approached.

I Am–I Am Not

On the Chart of Attitudes which accompanies the *Handbook for Preclears,* it will be found, at 22.0, I Am Myself.

The only true identity is "myself." It is not a name, it is not a designation. Orders, titles, ranks, praise and enduring fame, alike, do not bring about the condition I Am or an actual *identity.* They bring about, instead, an *identification* with all the liabilities of identification. The finality of identification is 0.0 or lower on the Tone Scale.

The concept of "infinite mind" is not new, but it has always been assigned to another beingness than self. The preclear who has sworn allegiance to some infinite beingness, and has then agreed that all space belonged to that beingness (and did not belong to self) and that the rights of creation and energy belonged to that beingness (and did not belong to self), will be found to be intensely aberrated. This is a handy and, to the very badly aberrated, acceptable method of denying any responsibility for anything. It is also the shortest route toward I Am Not. Infinite mind is individualistic. All Mankind does not depend upon or share a portion of the infinite mind.

On the contrary, the highest individualism attainable is the individualism of the infinite mind. It was beyond the power and grasp of the intellect, applying itself to the field of philosophy, to conceive a multiplicity of infinite minds. These commentators had agreed sufficiently with the MEST universe to conceive that the only space was the MEST universe space. And they could not understand that this was an illusion and that the existence of space does not depend upon existing space. Just as there can be an "infinity" of ideas, so can there be an "infinity" of "infinities" of space. Two beings, theoretically, each with an infinite mind and each capable of the production of an infinity of space, could yet co-produce sufficient space to communicate with each other. This may be difficult to conceive until one has attained a level of the Tone Scale sufficient for an expansive viewing of his potentialities, at which moment it becomes simplicity itself.

There is a psychosis which has as its manifestation the illusion that one is God and the ruler of the universe. This psychosis comes about from the effort of an individual, who is well below "complete agreement with the MEST universe," to shift into the valence of what he has already accepted to be the Creator of the universe. Instead of being himself, he has become unable even to be a MEST body in a sane condition, has conceived God to be MEST and has then shifted into the valence of God. God, in this case, will be found to be conceived to be a MEST object. As an aside to this, below the level of "complete agreement that the MEST universe is the only reality" begins the state which could be described by the statement, "I agree, I am still agreeing, and yet you are still punishing me." The unfortunate fact about the MEST universe is that it *is* MEST and is designed to punish and cares nothing about agreement with it—beyond the point that one agrees with it—and has no spirit of fair play whereby punishment ceases when one has acknowledged the winner.

Recognition of this brings on insanity in an effort to further back away from responsibility and further escape punishment. In the MEST universe, this escape from punishment is, of course, impossible. Thus, there is a level below 0.0 for any immortal being.

One of the first confusions on the part of the preclear which the auditor will encounter is the fact that the preclear considers himself to be in a state of I Am when he has a body and a name. This is high-tone compared to the Sub-zero state in which the thetan quite often finds himself, but it is very far from optimum. Here the preclear is confusing identity with his own sense of beingness. His sense of beingness does not depend upon and, indeed, is confused by a MEST identification, such as a name assigned to him and a body with which he can be recognized.

The society of Earth, to a large degree, has for structure "names" and "the ability to identify." The State finds itself very satisfied whenever it increases its ability to readily identify its citizenry and will resort to almost any pretext to collect the fingerprints and dossier of one and all.

Identity is such a liability and is so thoroughly MEST that individuality is really not possible in the presence of sharply defined identity. Reaching down into the Sub-zero Tone Scale, the thetan finds it expedient not only to mask his beingness, but to hide his identity with great thoroughness even from himself. This passion for non-identity is the spasm of clinging to the last shreds of individuality which would otherwise be lost. Thetans, from some of the corps operating in space, have thoroughly agreed to be amongst themselves completely black—the better to hide in the blackness of space. This blackness is found in the occluded case in many instances.

The commonest plea on the part of the preclear is "Who am I?"

He feels that if he could only answer this, he would be happy. He then ransacks his facsimiles for all of his past identities on his many spirals and as these amount to hundreds of millions, he finds no surcease. He succeeds only in damaging himself with the many injuries contained in the facsimiles through which he is searching. He is identifying to the point where he is searching not for the state of I Am, but for "What have I been labeled?" The attainment of the state I Am depends upon one's ability to again be able to create space, energy and objects, in and for his own universe, by himself or in cooperation with other thetans, and the rehabilitation of the many additional abilities of the thetan — for the creation of energy is but one of a very large number.

Thus the state of I Am is reached through Creative Processing and Postulate Processing, rather than the processing of MEST universe facsimiles or endless searching with an E-Meter to discover what one has been.

There are Gods above all other Gods and gods. Anything which has wide acceptance and has been successful, wherever suns shine and planets swing, is based upon some fundamental truth. There is no argument here against the existence of a Supreme Being or any devaluation intended. It is that amongst Gods, there are many false gods elected to power and position for the benefit and use of those who would control and make into the basest slaves the most sublime beings. As an early Greek said, "When one has examined the descriptions of God written by Man, he finds in that being, at best, a thirst for self-aggrandizement and adulation which would be disgusting in any man." Man has sought to make his God a "god of mud" because the early Greek, and even more distant peoples, made idols in the form of men by which they thought to entrap the beingness of some local divinity who troubled them.

More modern Man has fallen into the error of making God into the body of a Homo sapiens and posting him somewhere on high with a craving for vengeance and a pettiness in punishment matched only by the degradation of Homo sapiens himself.

There are Gods above all other Gods and Gods beyond the Gods of universes. But it were better, far better, to be a raving madman in his cell, than to be a thing with the ego, cruelty and jealous lust that base religions have set up to make men grovel down.

Win—Lose

It is noteworthy that as the preclear ascends the Tone Scale, his desire to win increases. Those low on the Tone Scale (even when they think they are trying to win) will almost uniformly set up their problems and solutions so that they will lose.

Homo sapiens has little conversation with true competence. There is an astonishing level of winningness above 4.0, where competence becomes a joy like poetry.

Regret of competence ensues when one has employed competence to injure another being drastically. The duelist begins with joy in competence of sword handling. And before long, because of the counter-emotion he receives from his practice of the art, conceives disgust for competence. In a later life he will carry this into everything he does, so fearing that he will employ competence to injure that he dares not practice competence in the smallest things. And, by failing to practice competence, so introduces losingness to the injury of himself and others. A man who instinctively recoils from competence and perfection at the wheel of a car, will sometimes cause an accident, rather than avoid one, if competence of a high order is required in the avoidance.

To win, one must wish to win.

When one no longer desires to win, one no longer desires to live.

Note:

The remaining three columns of the Chart of Attitudes (Start–Stop, Differences–Identification, Being–Had) are covered broadly in the earlier text.

∞

∞

Chapter Nineteen

THE CODE
OF HONOR

*"The unaberrated
individual
follows this code
more or less
instinctively."*

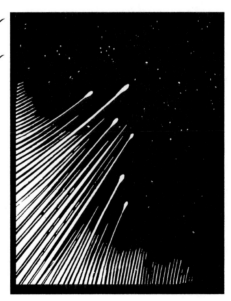

THE CODE OF HONOR

ELF-DETERMINISM'S basic intent as it goes up the Tone Scale is in the direction of a code. The unaberrated individual follows this code more or less instinctively. Every time it has been violated, it has been an aberration. This gives you some kind of a measure of aberration of a preclear and at the same time provides an ethic code which could actually be lived up to.

 Never desert a comrade in need, in danger or in trouble.

 Never withdraw allegiance once granted.

 Never desert a group to which you owe your support.

 Never disparage yourself or minimize your strength or power.

 Never need praise, approval or sympathy.

6 Never compromise with your own reality.

 7 Never permit your affinity to be alloyed.

 8 Do not give or receive communication unless you yourself desire it.

 9 Your self-determinism and your honor are more important than your immediate life.

 10 Your integrity to yourself is more important than your body.

 11 Never regret yesterday. Life is in you today and you make your tomorrow.

 12 Never fear to hurt another in a just cause.

 13 Don't desire to be liked or admired.

 14 Be your own adviser, keep your own counsel and select your own decisions.

 15 Be true to your own goals.

∞

References: Scientology 8-80

"...the moment he discovers himself as himself, as the source of energy and personality and beingness of a body, he becomes physically and mentally better."

∞

Chapter Twenty

THE EMOTIONAL SCALE AND SUB-ZERO TONE SCALE

"Below zero on the Tone Scale is applicable only to a thetan."

THE EMOTIONAL SCALE AND SUB-ZERO TONE SCALE

(Originally published in Scientology 8-80)

HE EMOTIONAL SCALE has been covered often and exhaustively elsewhere. As has been discussed in this text, it is dependent upon that characteristic of energy known as affinity — which itself is established by flows, dispersals and ridges.

Below zero on the Tone Scale is applicable only to a thetan.

It has been quite commonly observed that there are two positions for any individual on the Tone Scale. This occurs because there is a position for the composite of the thetan plus his MEST body, operating in a state of unknowingness that he is not a MEST body and behaving according to social patterns which give him some semblance of sanity. The other position on the Tone Scale is the position of the thetan himself and it is necessary for us to demonstrate a negative scale in order to find the thetan at all.

For the thetan, you will find the scale as follows:

Thetan Scale Range	40.0	Serenity of beingness
Well below	20.0	Action
body death	8.0	Exhilaration
at "0.0"	4.0	Enthusiasm
down to	3.0	Conservatism
complete	2.5	Boredom
unbeingness	2.0	Antagonism
as a thetan	1.8	Pain
	1.5	Anger
	1.2	No-sympathy
	1.0	Fear
	0.9	Sympathy
	0.8	Propitiation
	0.5	Grief
	0.375	Making amends
	0.05	Apathy
	0.0	Being a body
	−0.2	Being other bodies
	−1.0	Punishing other bodies
	−1.3	Responsibility as blame
	−1.5	Controlling bodies
	−2.2	Protecting bodies
	−3.0	Owning bodies
	−3.5	Approval from bodies
	−4.0	Needing bodies
	−8.0	Hiding

Thetan-Plus-Body

Social training and education sole guarantee of sane conduct

This Sub-zero Tone Scale shows that the thetan is several bands below knowingness as a body — and so he will be found in the majority of cases. In our Homo sapiens, he will be discovered to be below zero on the Tone Scale. The 0.0 to 4.0-plus Tone Scale was formulated on and referred to bodies and the activity of thetans with bodies. In order, then, to discover the state of mind of the thetan, one must examine the Sub-zero Scale. He has some trained patterns as a body which make it possible for him to *know* and to *be*. As himself, he has lost all beingness, all pride, all memories and all self-determined ability, but yet has an automatic-response mechanism in himself which continues furnishing his energy.

Each one of the above points on the scale is run as positive and negative!

Example: The beautiful sadness of needing bodies, the beautiful sadness of *not* needing bodies. The beauty of being responsible for bodies, the beauty of *not* being responsible for bodies. Each one is run as itself and then as the reverse with the addition of *not*.

The Sub-zero to 40.0 Scale is the range of the thetan. A thetan is lower than body death, since it survives body death. It is in a state of knowingness below 0.375 only when it is identifying itself as a body and *is,* to its own thinking, the body. The Body-Plus-Thetan Scale is from 0.0 to 4.0 and the position on this scale is established by the social environment and education of the composite being and is a stimulus-response scale. The preclear is initially above this 0.375 on the Body-Plus-Thetan range. Then, on auditing, he commonly drops from the false tone of the Body-Plus-Thetan Scale and into the true tone of the thetan.

This is actually the only self-determined tone present — the actual tone of the thetan. From this Sub-zero, he quickly rises upscale through the entire range, as a thetan, and generally settles at 20.0 and in command of the body and situations. The course of auditing, then, takes the preclear, quite automatically, down from the *false tone* of the Body-Plus-Thetan Scale to the *actual tone* of the thetan. Then the tone of the thetan rises back up the scale level by level.

It is not uncommon to find the preclear (who *is* the thetan) quite raving mad under the false "veneer" of social and educational stimulus-response training. And to discover that the preclear, while behaving quite normally in the Body-Plus-Thetan state, becomes irrational in the course of auditing. *But despite this,* the preclear is actually being far more sane and rational than ever before. And the moment he discovers himself as himself, as *the* source of energy and personality and beingness of a body, he becomes physically and mentally better. Thus the auditor must not be dismayed at the course of tone, but should simply persevere until he has the thetan up into rational range. A raving mad thetan is far more sane than a normal human being. But then, as you audit, observe it for yourself.

∞

Chapter Twenty-One

THE
DICHOTOMIES

*"A being
is apparently
an energy
production source."*

Chapter Twenty-One

$\mathcal{T}$HE
DICHOTOMIES

(Originally published in Scientology 8-80)

HILE THE AUDITOR can do much solely by reducing facsimiles, he soon will find that his preclears are not always able to erase facsimiles easily. He will find, occasionally, that he often has a difficult time when a particularly heavy facsimile is in restimulation. And do what he will, the auditor may find his preclear's tone remains unchanged and that the preclear's attitudes have not evolved to a better high.

We now come to "The Governor," mentioned in a lecture in the autumn of 1951. The speed of a preclear is the speed of his production of energy.

The most important step in establishing a preclear's self-determinism, the main goal of the auditor, is the rehabilitation of the preclear's ability to produce energy.

A being is apparently an energy production source. How does he produce live energy without mechanical means, cellular activity, or food?

The basic principle of energy production by a being has been copied in electronics. It is very simple. A difference of potential of two areas can establish an energy flow of themselves. Carbon batteries, electric generators and other producers of electrical flows act on the principle that a difference of energy potential in two or more areas can cause an electrical impulse to flow between or amongst them.

The preclear is static and kinetic, meaning he is no-motion and motion. These, interplaying, produce electrical flow.

A preclear, as a static, can hold two or more energy flows of different wavelengths in proximity and between them obtain a flow.

A preclear can hold a difference of flow between two waves and a static so long (and arduously) that the effect of a discharging condenser can be obtained. This can "explode" a facsimile.

The preclear flows electrical currents of command at the body. These hit pre-established ridges (areas of dense waves) and cause the body to perceive or act. The preclear takes perception from the body with tractor beams. He holds the body still or braces himself against it by wrapping a "tractor" (pulling) beam around it while he places a "pressor" (pushing) beam at his back to command himself into action. (You can almost break a preclear's spine by asking him to contact his own tractor around his body and yet withhold the pressor against his spine.)

All an auditor really needs to know about this is the elementary method of using a difference of potential. That creates energy.

The only thing wrong with a preclear with an aged MEST body is that he has too many facsimiles of his tractors and pressors handling his own MEST body. And the rickety state of the body feeds back "slowness" so that he thinks his energy is low and, until worked with some method such as this, facsimiles do not reduce.

Any difference of potential, played one against the other, creates energy. Aesthetic waves against a static produce energy. Aesthetic waves against analytical waves produce energy. Analytical waves against emotional waves produce energy. Emotional waves against effort waves produce energy. Effort against matter produces energy.

The last is the method used on Earth in generating electrical current for power. The others are equally valid and produce even higher flows. This is a gradient scale of beingness, from the zero–infinity of theta to the solidity of matter.

The differences of potential most useful are easy to run.

This is, actually, alternating current (AC) running. There can be DC running or chain fission running, but these are very experimental at this writing.

AC is created by the static holding first one, then the other, of a dichotomy of two differences of potential. A flow is run in one direction with one of the pair, then in the other direction with the other.

The dichotomies are:

1. Survive
   Succumb
2. Affinity
   No affinity
3. Communication
   No communication
4. Agree
   Disagree
5. Start
   Stop
6. Be
   Not be
7. Know
   Know not
8. Cause
   Effect
9. Change
   No change
10. Win
    Lose
11. I am
    I am not
12. Faith
    Distrust
13. Imagine
    Truth
14. Believe
    Not believe
15. Always
    Never
16. Future
    Past

17. Everybody
    Nobody
18. Owns all
    Owns nothing
19. Responsible
    Not responsible
20. Right
    Wrong
21. Stay
    Escape
22. Beauty
    Ugliness
23. Reason
    Emotion
24. Emotion
    Effort
25. Effort
    Apathy
26. Acceptance
    Rejection
27. Sane
    Insane
28. No-sympathy
    Sympathy
29. Sympathy
    Propitiation

And the state of Static, a motionlessness sometimes necessary to run.

How are these used?

One asks the preclear to flow agreement, then disagreement. He flows a feeling, a thought (never the phrase!) of "agreement," out or in, in the direction he chooses relative to himself. He lets this flow until it turns smoky gray or white, then black. Then he changes the direction of flow and gets the thought or feeling of "disagreement." He runs this until it turns gray or white, then black. When this has turned black or dark, he again runs "agreement" in its direction until he gets gray or white, then again black. Now he reverses the flow and flows the thought "disagreement" until he gets gray or white, then blackness. And so on and on.

It will be noted that at first it may take some little time for a flow to run from black through white to black. As the preclear continues to run, after minutes of many hours, he begins to run faster, then faster and faster, until at last he can keep a flow blazing and crackling.

A method of aberrating beings was to give them white and black energy sources in their vicinity. These show up on a very low-tone occluded case as blazing white and shining white. That is an electronic incident, not his own energy flow. These run blazing white *in one direction* for minutes or hours before they go black. They then run the other way, blazing white, almost as long.

When black predominates in such incidents, they do not diminish or reduce. Ask the preclear, in such a case, to do what he "has to do" to get the incident all white.

As the preclear runs, he finds the speed of the change of flow changes more and more rapidly until it runs like a vibration.

This vibration, theoretically, can increase to a strong current which becomes so great it is well to *ground* your preclear by using an E-Meter or letting him hold a wire in each hand which is connected to a bare water pipe or radiator. Otherwise, his MEST body may be damaged by the flow.

Run a dichotomy only against its mate. Run in alternating directions until the flow turns black.

Don't run a black "flow." It doesn't flow or run out.

∞

Part Two

Methods of Running

"If one
were to leave
the MEST universe,
one would solely
create space
of his own..."

Chapter Twenty-Two

METHODS
OF RUNNING

"There are
many methods of
running facsimiles
and handling
ridges and flows."

Chapter Twenty-Two

$\mathscr{M}$ETHODS
OF RUNNING

$\mathscr{T}$HERE ARE MANY methods of running facsimiles and handling ridges and flows. These have been covered in other publications. All of them have validity and can advance cases.

In the present publication, there are only two processes which are stressed and these processes are superior to others published prior to December 1, 1952. A great many tests have established the fact that two processes, both of them simple, produce far better results than any of the others.

The title *Scientology 8-8008* means:

The attainment of infinity (8) by the reduction of the MEST universe's apparent infinity (8) to zero (0) and the increase of the zero (0) of one's own universe to an infinity (8) of one's own universe.

This road is attained by Postulate Processing and Creative Processing.

To run any incident or use any process, it is necessary for the auditor to have a very sound idea of what he is doing. And, to this end, it is recommended that he know and be able to use the following processes.

PROCESSING:

The Code of Ethics (Honor)

The Thetan

The Entities

Running Engrams

Running Secondaries

Running Locks

Concepts and Feelings

Running Ridges (Circuits)

Running Live Flow

Freeing the Thetan by Concept and Feeling

Freeing the Thetan by Present and Future

Randomity

Freeing by Dichotomies

Freeing by Tone Scale

Freeing the Thetan by Orientation

Freeing the Thetan by Positioning and Exhaustion of Flows

∞

Chapter Twenty-Three

CREATIVE PROCESSING

*"The ability
to perceive the
MEST universe is
the ability to agree."*

CREATIVE PROCESSING

THE WHOLE OF the data covered in this volume is utilized in Creative Processing.

When one has mastered the component parts of the mind and the interrelationships of space, energy, items and experience, he will find Creative Processing surprisingly easy to apply and productive of very swift results. The goal of this process is the rehabilitation of as much of the thetan's capabilities as is possible, to permit him to utilize or be free of bodies as he chooses, and even, in lesser magnitude, to rid the preclear of psychosomatics, eradicate compulsions, obsessions and inhibitions to raise his reaction time and intelligence level.

This process does whatever has been previously intended by earlier processes, utilizing a knowledge of these in order to assess the state of the preclear and in order to parallel his difficulty with creation, change and destruction of mock-ups.

Gradient Scales

Gradient scales are vitally necessary in the application of Creative Processing. The term "gradient scale" can apply to anything and means "a scale of condition graduated from zero to infinity." Absolutes are considered to be unobtainable.

Depending on the direction the scale is graduated, there could be an infinity of wrongness and an infinity of rightness. Thus, the gradient scale of rightness would run from the theoretical (but unobtainable) zero of rightness up to the theoretical infinity of rightness. A gradient scale of wrongness would run from a zero of wrongness to an infinity of wrongness.

The word "gradient" is meant to define "lessening or increasing degrees of condition." The difference between one point on a gradient scale and another point could be as different or as wide as the entire range of the scale itself. Or it could be as tiny as to need the most minute discernment for its establishment.

The gradient scale of the creation of a being would be (but in Creative Processing generally is not) concerned with time.

In Creative Processing, the gradient scale as it would refer to the creation of a person could be, first, the envisionment of an area where the person might have been or might be, then the envisionment of an area the person commonly frequented, the creation of a footprint the person had made, and then perhaps some article of apparel or a possession such as a handkerchief. The creative steps would then continue, until more and more of a person was established, and at last the entire person would have been created.

Likewise, in the destruction of a person, the gradient scale could (but generally would not) begin with blowing him up or making him grow old. If the auditor finds the preclear diffident about destroying an illusion of some person, the environment can first be diminished slightly, then perhaps the person's shadow might be shortened and so on, until the entire person could be destroyed.

The essence of gradient scale work is to do as much creation, change and destruction, in terms of illusion, as the preclear can accomplish with confidence. And to go from successful step to greater step until an entire success in destruction, alteration or creation (or their companion states of experience, such as start, change and stop) is accomplished.

The mind works easily if led through successive successes into a complete confidence. The mind can be confused and set back enormously by demanding that it do too much too fast. Much can be accomplished by requesting of the mind that it do small portions of the task. This does not mean that processing should go slowly or that illusions that are easy to create, change or destroy should have much time spent on them. It does mean that as soon as an auditor has established a disability on the part of the preclear in creating illusions of certain places, persons, conditions, things, colors or any other thing in this or any other universe, he approaches the subject gradually, by gradient scale. And by accomplishing repeated successes with the preclear, of greater and greater magnitude, finally achieving a complete "banishment" of the disability.

Agreements

The reason a preclear cannot alter a postulate, or change or start or stop, lies in the influence upon him of his agreements and experiences in the MEST universe and other universes. To run out these agreements and experiences, as such, would be in part to agree with them over again.

The mind is actually quite free to alter postulates and change its own condition if permitted to do so at a speed that it finds comfortable. The mind will not take wide divergences which seem to it to tend toward its own diminishment or destruction.

It was by a gradient scale of agreement that he came at last to accept and very nearly succumb to the MEST universe itself. The build-up of illusion was so slow and insidious that only the closest assessment would reveal to the preclear and the auditor how far these tiny steps of agreement led at last. The motto of the MEST universe could be said to be: "Thou shalt have no force nor illusion, nor thine own space or self-made energy or thing, for all illusion is mine and with that thou shalt agree. If thou art, I shall not be."

By a series of minute agreements, the preclear has at last given up all his own belief in his ability to make a universe or even to create and maintain a minor illusion. He does not know or even suspect that he is capable of producing illusions sufficiently strong to be observable by others (and if he thought this were true, he would attribute it to some mysterious thing) and so short and final are the punishments of the MEST universe, he would tend to shy away from this. But upon his ability to create illusions depends the very existence of all his hopes and dreams and any beauty he will ever see or feel. In truth, all sensation which he believes to come from these masses of illusory energy, known as the MEST universe, are first implanted through agreement upon what he is to perceive and then perceived again by himself—with the step hidden that he has extended his own sensation to be felt and perceived by himself. He is fully convinced that the MEST universe itself has sensation which it can deliver to him, whereas all the MEST universe has is an enforced agreement which, though of no substance, yet by a gradient scale, came to be an illusion which seems very masterful to a preclear.

To prove the reality and solidity of the MEST universe, the preclear could pound his fist upon a desk and demonstrate that his fist hit something. He is making, again, the error of implanting sensation and not knowing he has implanted it.

For the fist which he pounds on the desk is a MEST universe fist consisting of MEST universe energy, which is itself a MEST universe agreement. And it is meeting a desk, which is itself a MEST universe agreement. And he is only demonstrating that when the MEST universe is perceived to impact upon the MEST universe, one can then implant a realistic impact and reperceive it for his own wonderful edification.

"Reality," then, is a delusion, because it is one's own illusion which has been disowned by one and is then received by one as being another thing. Only by shedding all responsibility for one's own energy can one fall into this covert trap. If one is unwilling to be responsible for energy, he is capable of using energy and then not perceiving that he uses it. One who blames others continually can be discovered to effect most of the things for which he is blaming other people. In such a way an individual, with the "very best MEST universe Mark 10,000 ears," takes no responsibility for having implanted the sensation of sound in order to receive the sensation of sound. A preclear, as he comes up the Tone Scale, more and more often catches himself doing this. And even though he does not know the principle involved (for no preclear has to be educated in Scientology to receive benefit from it), he recognizes that, even in the case of a loud crash, his continuation of association from his environment permits him to perceive with others that a crash of objects has taken place, which he with others continuously re-creates solidly, and that he must actually cause for his own perception the sound of the crash.

In that the beingness of an individual is actually extended for miles in all directions around him, if not much further, any idea or thought or past thought (as there is no past) is part of his beingness and so he must continually strive to be "faithful to his agreements with the MEST universe."

To undo this state of affairs, it is only necessary to rehabilitate the awareness of the preclear that he himself is capable of creating illusions. As he rehabilitates this facility, the preclear, without any coaching or evaluation on the part of the auditor, begins to recognize that his viewpoint is expanding and that he is becoming all pervasive (but that he can collect his awareness at any point) and that the "brutal reality" all around him is continuously manufactured by himself out of agreements and association with other viewpoints. So long as he is fixed in a condition where he is in agreement with all spaces and viewpoints, he sees and feels automatically with all other viewpoints. He is about the level of energy, if one can use the term, "on the same wavelength" with all other beingness—a condition which does not permit differentiation. As he rehabilitates his abilities in independent creation, he can change this "wavelength" at will and can go into or out of agreement with all other points of beingness. The matter of perceiving then becomes entirely a matter of self-choice.

It is, for instance, quite startling to a preclear to discover that as soon as he is free of the ridges of the body (which is to say, when he has discovered he can change his viewpoint) that he is already partly out of agreement with other viewpoints and that the MEST universe becomes slightly jumbled. He is apt to be very anxious about this, for it is in conflict with the agreements to which he is subject. He immediately may struggle very hard to regain a state of affairs whereby he can view the MEST universe as everyone else views it. Indeed, the auditor must continually be on guard to prevent the preclear from attempting to re-assume these agreements.

A badly trained auditor can always be identified by the fact that he shares the preclear's anxiety that the preclear view the environment as the environment "should be."

The reason why a non-cleared auditor does not do well with these processes is that he is very anxious for the preclear to continue agreement with all others and to perceive the surroundings as exactly, when exteriorized, as he did when he was looking through MEST eyes and perceptions (which is to say, when the preclear was at his exact agreed-upon point of viewpoint). The ability to perceive the MEST universe is the ability to agree. The preclear's accuracy of perception of the MEST universe is of no consequence.

An auditor can act to permit or even encourage a preclear to try to "see," "feel" and "hear" the MEST universe, when exteriorized, long before the preclear is prepared to do so with equanimity. The auditor, when doing this, is dramatizing his own urge to agree with viewpoints and perceive. A preclear, who exteriorizes readily, may find with a shock that he is not perceiving the MEST universe as he commonly supposes it should be perceived and quickly goes back into his body to reassure himself that he is "keeping his contract of agreement." If the auditor demands that the preclear perceive the environment when exteriorized, then the auditor will discover that the preclear will drop in tone and that, when he has gone into his body once more, a great deal of patient auditing is necessary to regain the preclear's confidence in himself. The preclear exteriorizing may find himself in all sorts of space and time tie-ups, for he has insufficient command of space and energy to independently sort out viewpoints when unassisted by the orientation of the MEST body itself—which is, of course, in debased and degraded agreement of a very set nature.

Shuns

There are two "shuns." These are *invalidation* and *evaluation*.

The auditor must eschew them vigorously.

The major invalidation which could be practiced, in using Scientology 8-8008, would be a demand that the preclear see the environment as it is seen through MEST perception or to criticize him for not being able to do so. The majority of the preclear's perceptions may be correct, but some percentage of his perception is going to be enough "off wavelength" with other agreement viewpoints to cause him to perceive strangely.

After a very large amount of auditing, even as much as fifty hours (when the preclear has regained his ability to create, with considerable solidity, his own illusions), it will be found that the preclear can at will perceive the MEST universe and can do so with accuracy. He can further (without the aid of a body) move objects, heal at a distance and do a thousand other "interesting tricks" which could very well be viewed with considerable awe. For they have not been seen on Earth in recorded history, but have lived in legend.

Procedure

Using Standard Operating Procedure, Issue 3 (SOP 3), as given in this volume, the auditor yet takes a very thorough assessment of his preclear with an E-Meter (see *Preclear Assessments: Creation and Destruction*).

He discovers, in accordance with information in this book, what the preclear is unable to:

Start	*Change*	*Stop*
Create	*Alter*	*Destroy*
Be	*Do*	*Have*
Differentiate	*Associate*	*Identify*

on each and every one of the eight dynamics and their component parts. The auditor makes a complete list. This is the "Can't List."

Exteriorized, if possible, or interiorized as in the later numbered steps (see SOP 3), the preclear is then made to mock-up illusions about each one of these Can'ts and to change the size, character and position of the illusions (or any part thereof) in space, shift it in time (simply by knowing it has been shifted by him), until at last the preclear is able to handle the whole object of the Can't with complete facility. Can'ts may be inability to destroy women or snakes or specific persons, or create machinery, or write legibly. The preclear is requested to accomplish, by illusions, the smallest gradient of the Can't with which he can successfully start. And under auditing direction—by moving this small portion of the whole here and there in space, tipping it this way and that and making it, in particular, disobey "natural laws" in the MEST universe—the preclear is led to an ability to create or destroy the Can't.

The Can't is also the "Must." Can't is an inhibition. Must is an enforcement. What *must* the preclear do and what must be done to him? By what? By Creative Processing and gradient scales, he achieves mock-ups until each one of these Musts becomes a "Can if I want to, but don't have to."

There are also the "Desires." These are the cravings for sensation, or possession or identification, which brought the preclear into and made him continue agreements. Behind every case, the Desires are paramount and of greater importance than the Can'ts. Why does he desire bodies? Why is his Second Dynamic aberrated? Why does he feel he cannot be free? Can he differentiate between his own actual wantingness and the wantingness of MEST itself, which is trying to have *him*? The Desires are resolved by Creative Processing, wherein the preclear does mock-ups of the necessary acts which he desires or the necessary behaviors which brought him into agreement, until he can at last laugh at them.

In that Creative Processing does not take long in terms of time, the assessment list can afford to be very broad and to cover every possible phase through the system of the dynamics and the cycles-of-action.

This is a list of things the preclear must be able to do with an illusion:

Create the condition, energy or object

Conserve it

Protect it

Control it

Hide it

Change it

Age it

Make it go backwards on a cycle-of-action

Perceive it with all perceptions

Shift it at will in time

Rearrange it

Duplicate it

Turn it upside down or on the side at will

Make it disobey MEST *laws*

Be it

Not be it

Destroy it

In order to accomplish these things—if the whole of any condition cannot be fulfilled—by gradient scale some tiny portion of the condition must be fulfilled. When a small condition has been fulfilled, the condition is then enlarged until the whole condition can be fulfilled.

CHAPTER TWENTY-THREE
CREATIVE PROCESSING

That preclear who cannot get even a shadow of an illusion, so that he can perceive it in any manner, must be coaxed to see white spots, black spots (of his own creation) and to change these in space and time, enlarge and contract them, until he has a certain command and control of black and white. This must be done, with such a preclear, without regard to the number of hours it takes or the patience of the drill. It can be done with the eyes open or shut, whichever the preclear finds best.

When the preclear is discovered to be trying to prevent a motion or condition, the auditor should magnify that very condition with new mock-ups related to it, i.e., if objects keep rushing in on the preclear, mock-up objects rushing in until the action is enormously magnified but under the preclear's complete control. If the preclear cannot start something, make him stop it. If he cannot reverse a direction, make him change the nature of the object (which he is trying to reverse) enough times to permit him to reverse the original disability. If the preclear cannot create something, have him create anything even vaguely associated with it and, by association, at last have him mock-up the actual thing.

The essence of Creative Processing is moving objects in space when they have been mocked-up.

They are moved near and far, to the right, left, behind the preclear, below his feet, above his head and in front of him. He must know that he has changed the location of the object. If he cannot make a large change of location, have him do a small change of location. If he cannot do a small change of location, have him alter the object by turning it different colors, or by enlarging or contracting it, or by pushing it away or bringing it near him, until he can make it move sideways. In failing to do this, have him do a change with some allied object.

The essence of Creative Processing is a continuation of success.

Be careful not to give the preclear things which make him fail. Do not let his failures mount up. Estimate the preclear and pay attention to what he is doing. Find out from him, continually, the condition of his illusions (if you yourself, as an auditor, cannot see them). Putting objects into yesterday or tomorrow, or well into the future or into the past, is vitally necessary to processing.

Control of the illusion is the essence of commands.

The preclear must be able to:

Create, Grow, Conserve, Decay and Destroy

Start, Change and Stop

Be, Do and Have

Differentiate, Associate and Identify

Handle in Space, with Energy and in Time

any object, actual or mythical, in all the eight dynamics and with high preference given to anything which disobeys "natural laws" of the MEST universe.

That auditor with a high order of imagination, who is himself Clear, finds mock-ups very easy to "think up" and request to the preclear. But it is not necessary to have such an imagination as a routine assessment will discover immediately that the most ordinary things fall into the Can't, Must and Desire brackets in the preclear's life.

The preclear will be discovered, on the First Dynamic, quite ordinarily not able to create, change or destroy (especially destroy) his own body or bodies in which he thinks he is encased within his own body (old time track bodies such as a Fifth Invader Force body). He will be found to be incapable, in many directions, with facsimiles, communication lines and other matters on the First Dynamic alone. On the Second Dynamic, many incapabilities will come to view. And so on, along all the dynamics. On the Fifth Dynamic, he will quite ordinarily be found to be incapable of handling snakes, spiders, vicious fish, bacteria, wild animals, domestic pets. On the Seventh Dynamic, he will be discovered unable to handle other thetans, even in the most elementary fashion of bringing two dots of light into proximity and then separating them (an exercise which blows head ridges, in many preclears, quite explosively). On the Eighth Dynamic, his limitations quite ordinarily become too obvious for comment. But on each and every dynamic, he must be able to do any of the above cycles or conditions.

Cleared Theta Clear

Standard Operating Procedure tells how to exteriorize a thetan. Creative Processing, Rising Scale Processing, Postulate Processing are then necessary to bring him toward a state of a Cleared Theta Clear.

The state of *Theta Clear* simply demands that the preclear remains outside his body when the body is hurt. And the state is adequate to prevent his being trapped again by a body, except in unusual circumstances. There is no guarantee of long continuance in the condition.

The state of *Cleared Theta Clear* is, however, another thing. For it means a person who is able to create his own universe or, living in the MEST universe, is able to create illusions perceivable by others at will, to handle MEST universe objects without mechanical means and to have and feel no need of bodies or even the MEST universe to keep himself and his friends interested in existence.

∞

POSTULATE PROCESSING

"Actually, energy is produced by the thetan simply by postulating that it will be in existence."

POSTULATE PROCESSING

CTUALLY, ENERGY IS produced by the thetan simply by postulating that it will be in existence. What he says will be so, becomes so for him. If he becomes extremely powerful, it becomes so for others. This condition has been misused by most thetans who, often in the past, have been afraid of making postulates that will come true. They believe that if they say a thing will happen, it will happen — to such an extent that they now revulse against stating anything will happen.

Another aberrative condition with regard to postulates is that for the sake of randomity, the thetan at some time or another has set up the postulate that every time he makes a postulate, a reverse postulate will occur which he will not know about — in such a way that he can "play chess with himself" without spoiling the game by knowing what his left hand is doing when his right hand makes a move.

It is not true that postulates have to be located all through the facsimiles and worn out by repetition. It is just as easy to make new postulates. But first one must recover the power from the depths to which his postulates have taken him. The most dangerous postulates are those postulates where he decided to "agree" with something which would become aberrative.

You can see by examination of any facsimile in the preclear, related to an accident that the most aberrative things in that facsimile are what the preclear himself decided.

Postulates are accompanied by evaluations and conclusions. It is often possible to "loosen" a postulate by discovering to the preclear why he made it or what data he was using at the time.

As a preclear becomes very aberrated and believes himself to be more and more MEST, his postulates become as unwieldy to use as actual objects and he finds them as difficult to change.

When doing Creative Processing, and moving objects and energy in created space and time, it comes as a shock to some preclears that they are handling time by shifting space. The preclear is doing this by making postulates. One handles time by simply saying that he had a thing and now does not have it, or that he will have or will view a thing in the future. One does not shift time by shifting space, nor does one continue to look at something he has put into the past. He says it is in the past and so it becomes in the past.

When the thetan is unable to handle postulates about time, the auditor should ask him about some MEST universe incidents, such as breakfast. And then inquire, How he remembered that he had breakfast? And, If he will have something to eat on the morrow? And then, How he knows he will have something to eat on the morrow? He does not look at his breakfast to find out if he had breakfast. He *knows* that he ate breakfast. And he does not go into tomorrow to find out if he will probably eat on the morrow. He knows, or at least believes it possible, that he will eat on the morrow. Moving time (as in any other postulate) is knowingness, not viewingness. An object goes into the past in the same space as it was in, in the present, and in the future may be in the same space as it was in the past.

The space does not change. The condition of havingness changes and one estimates this by some degree of knowingness.

The entire subject of postulates is the subject of certainty and self-belief. That preclear who has a low self-belief finds it difficult, first, to make a postulate which he will believe and, second, to undo one he has made. Creative Processing and Postulate Processing alike remedy this.

Rising Scale Processing

Rising Scale Processing is another way of doing Postulate Processing. One takes any point or column of the Chart of Attitudes (as given in this text) which the preclear can reach and asks the preclear, then, to shift his postulate upwards toward a higher level.

In order to do this, the auditor says:

"Now, on the subject of rightness and wrongness, how wrong do you think you generally are?"

The preclear tells him. The auditor says:

"How high can you shift this attitude toward believing yourself right?"

The preclear shifts the attitude as high as he can. The auditor takes this as the next level from which he will work upward until he attains, as nearly as possible, a postulate which will "hold" to the effect that the preclear believes himself right.

Rising Scale Processing should not be confused with the processing of flows. One can process all these columns in terms of flows. Rising Scale Processing is simply a method of shifting postulates upward, toward optimum, from where the preclear believes he is on the chart.

Rising Scale Processing is essentially a process directed toward increasing belief in self, by using all the "buttons" on the Chart of Attitudes.

The preclear is generally found to be quite uncertain about his postulates. He does not know whether or not what he says will take effect or, if he says it and if it takes effect, if it will rebound against him. He becomes afraid to make postulates for fear he will make some postulate destructive to himself or others and may even discover himself making postulates to convince himself he should be ill.

One has to tell oneself what to *be* before one *is*. Recovery of this ability is the essence of processing a thetan.

Postulate Processing is a very vital process to apply to the thetan. When he is exteriorized, he can change his postulates rapidly. If he finds himself thinking slowly and doing other things which are not optimum when he is outside, one can better his situation and condition by asking him to change postulates.

Chapter Twenty-Five

THE ANATOMY
OF SPACE

*"The preclear
has a viewpoint
and is the center
of that viewpoint."*

Chapter Twenty-Five

THE ANATOMY OF SPACE

BEFORE ENERGY CAN exist in this universe, space must exist. His inability to create space is one of the most aberrative characteristics of the thetan whom we find in a MEST body. He has become reduced to a point, even in his own concept, and perhaps even less than a point. For he has no space of his own, but must depend upon bodies and other conditions to believe he has space.

It is of the utmost importance for the auditor to understand space. Space can be considered to be a "viewpoint of dimension." It does not matter how many dimensions there are or what conditions are set up for these dimensions in space. In the MEST universe, throughout all of its galaxies, it has only length, breadth and depth. Space warps and other things of equal interest can exist in one's own universe. But they do not exist as such, evidently, in the MEST universe.

The assignation of dimension is the essence of space. But even before dimension can be assigned, one must have viewpoint. If one is assigning dimension from his viewpoint, he is cause. If dimension is being assigned to his viewpoint, he is effect. He is cause or effect to the degree that he can assign dimension and call it space.

The preclear has a viewpoint and is the center of that viewpoint. Splitting his attention often finds him occupying several viewpoints. He is capable of assuming many. Where he is "aware of being aware" is, however, his central viewpoint. And although this may be communicated with or interlocked to some other viewpoint which he could call his own (here on Earth or even on some other planet), he is yet, as himself, the center of assignation of dimensions *where* he is and *as* he is.

In many preclears this becomes so blurred that he does not know whether he is in or out of the body. Here, even the center of viewpoint has been overridden by MEST assignation of dimension.

An essential in the agreement to any illusion is the acceptance of the dimensions it assigns or that one may assign to it. Space is no more complicated than this. But when a preclear has been overridden by enforced assignation of dimension to an enormous degree, his own viewpoint may be found to be scattered and dispersed. It is this condition which finds the preclear unable to tell whether he is in or out of his body. When this condition exists, he is in the state of being incapable of confronting the MEST universe even to the point of asserting the ownership of a viewpoint.

The solution to this problem is simple in principle, although it may be many hours in auditing solution. Where the preclear has a certainty of center of viewpoint, he exteriorizes immediately and can become a Theta Clear in a very few hours. When he has been compressed by counter-efforts and emotions into an acceptance of MEST dimension to the point where he cannot even be certain of viewpoint, it is necessary to recover this center of viewpoint in order to recover a point from which space can be assigned and (even more importantly to the auditor) where the preclear can be exteriorized easily and in a knowing condition.

One of the first "tricks" in auditing is to get the preclear to look from the center of his head at his environment and the room. He very often sees it clearly and as it is and, by this, does adjust his vision to see through his ridges. Even an occluded case can sometimes do this and can then be exteriorized rapidly. The next "trick" is to find some segment of the environment which the preclear can see. And then to ask him, What is in the areas where he can see nothing or does not wish to see? He will say this or that, maybe, in these areas. The auditor then has him create these things, or change these things and shift these things (which he is afraid may be in these areas) until he is no longer interested, at which time he can envision the actual surroundings. By continuing this "trick" of rehabilitation of potential occupation of space (for a preclear will not occupy space which he considers dangerous) the preclear may be found to exteriorize suddenly and, sometimes, with violence. In such a case, he believes himself to be occupying yet another space (hiding, perhaps, in the darkness of deep MEST space) as well as in a body. Routine Orientation and Creative Processing remedy this.

By making the preclear alter the body he is occupying, making mock-ups which he superimposes and changes around in disagreement with the MEST universe, upside down and right side up, he becomes better able to have a viewpoint from which he can create space and from which he can at least handle MEST universe space.

The preclear who does not exteriorize readily is not sure he is here at all. And, indeed, he may be co-occupying other areas. A study of the preclear with the E-Meter, locating him in other spaces and bringing him into the space where he is being audited, can best be done with Creative Processing — not by running facsimiles, for these only make him disperse even further.

This preclear often has difficulties with time and has space confused with time. Time is not handled by moving space. Time is handled simply by *having* and *not-having*. The MEST universe insists that anything that disappears must have gone somewhere. Thus the preclear is saddled with the belief that he must create space to put things in whenever time changes. Having the preclear conceive time change in the space which he occupies, by refusing to let him go on *looking* at it in yesterday or to see it in tomorrow, but simply making him *know* that it is now in yesterday and the space is the same, does much to rehabilitate his orientation.

Drills in which space is assigned are highly beneficial to any preclear and particularly so to those preclears who do not exteriorize readily or who cannot easily find themselves when they are out of their body. Simply have the preclear "disagree" with dimensions around him, and see them with purposeful, creative distortion, and he will at length focalize his viewpoint so that he can handle space and *know* that he is the center.

A being can be knowingly in many places, but being scattered into many places unknowingly is the worst of conditions.

∞

Chapter Twenty-Six

GENERAL PROCESSING

"Earth could be considered to be, at this time, an egress terminal."

GENERAL PROCESSING

NYTHING WHICH REHABILITATES the self-determinism of a preclear—whether education, change of environment, running facsimiles, Theta Clearing or the creation of one's own universe—is valid processing. Any one of these will raise the Tone Scale of the preclear markedly.

At the end of 80,000 hours of investigation of beingness in the MEST universe, I have concluded that these processes, which make it possible for the preclear to disagree with the MEST universe, also make it possible for him to handle the MEST universe, or to create his own, or be part of a group which creates a universe—as the case may be.

Scientology 8-8008 is remarkable for its ability to better the beingness and action potentials of the individual. It is, sadly enough, the only technique which I have seen produce excellent and fast results in the hands of trained auditors. Part of the reason is that the auditors who are trained in Scientology, at this time, must be themselves Theta Clears. But this is not all of the reason. Homo sapiens has and will continue to use any technique delivered into his hands for the control and enslavement of others. For Homo sapiens is frightened.

Even when an auditor was competent with earlier techniques, it would often occur that his preclear would return into his past environment and would relapse. This occurred because others had a vested interest in the preclear's continuation in a state of aberration and others would lose no moment in starting again to crush this preclear down the Tone Scale to a point where they conceived he was more easily controlled. MEST is the most easily controlled item in the MEST universe and the closer a human being could be pressed toward MEST, the easier it was thought to control him. That his value and ethical sense deteriorated in direct ratio to the degree he was depressed down the Tone Scale was overlooked by the Homo sapiens who had a passion for slavery.

The primary benefit of Scientology 8-8008 is that it works so swiftly, even when indifferently used, that the persons in the environment of the preclear are overreached rapidly by the preclear and find themselves subject to his control when they act to continue his aberration. Further, the auditor is seldom aware of the height his preclear attains until the preclear attains it.

Processing has always worked in the hands of a competent auditor and it was better for any technique, no matter how dangerous, to be known to Man if it could benefit at least a few. For Homo sapiens had no psychotherapy. In Dianetics, he had his first thoroughly validated psychotherapy. And Dianetics worked and still works, uniformly, in the hands of those skilled in its application. In Scientology in general and in Theta Clearing in particular, the upper limits of Homo sapiens, as such, have been transcended. And it would not be good semantics to call a Theta Clear a "Homo sapiens" or even, exactly speaking, a "person." For he is a thetan, with a body he uses for purposes of action and communication, and his viewpoint is quite altered.

His general health is more or less directly under his control. But there is no goal for the body as a final goal in Scientology, for the body is a tool. The genetic entity which built the human body *really* wanted to be served. The complexities and ridges, which he developed, speak of a craving for energy and self-service which could only be the basest aberration. And, true enough, the genetic entity is aberrated almost beyond belief, as any thetan discovers when he seeks to clear the genetic entity. The body is quite alive and self-motivated without the thetan, as the thetan soon discovers. But it is so used to taking orders from successive lines of thetans (which themselves, someday, would probably become part of this complex system of ridges) that its "mental activities" are quite stupid. The thetan, who has lived in this association and has believed himself to be the body, is early quite appalled at the character of the genetic entity — who is cowardly, a thing of stimulus-response, without further will or goals than to grow a body and obsessed entirely with the idea of growing one.

The thetan can repair the body quite easily, if he so chooses, but he quite often sees it as a pointless activity. For one's personality is not even faintly dependent upon the body, but is only debased by association with one. When one has learned to control a body from a distance, he is usually content to let it get along as best it can. For the reduction of all counter-efforts of the genetic entity would be a reduction of the entire body. The genetic entity has his whole track and has had his travails.

In other parts of space, not too incredibly, "dolls" are used by thetans — things which can be animated easily by theta energy and which are disposable and which do not have the uncomfortable circumstance of being, themselves, any more alive than any other MEST.

The MEST universe, itself, has a considerable cravingness in it. It is composed of energy which was emanated in order to "have." And the energy still contains as its basic characteristic "have" and "not-have" and is itself, when contacted, found to possess a craving—which does not make the MEST alive, but which speaks of that which made the MEST. This cravingness is an essential part of all matter. Certain metals contain the desire to "be had" much more than others. And certain other metals contain the craving "not to be had." This is one way of looking at positive and negative reactions. The body, being composed of such energy, makes it feel as though it is holding on to the thetan. Nothing is really holding on to the thetan as he has no substance which can be held. Even the genetic entity does not hold on to the thetan, but probably considers him some sort of far-off commanding god—if he thinks of him at all.

Space has its own demanding quality and insists on its dimensions being accepted by anything in the universe. For it was erected and is erected on a command basis in the MEST universe.

Processing must resolve this havingness on the part of matter and the commandingness on the part of space. To confront these directly is, for most preclears, an impossibility. For it only drives them further into an apathy of agreement with MEST. The preclear has long contested with the MEST universe and has continually sought to create his own universe, only to find the MEST universe declaring itself stronger each time and compressing the illusion to nothing.

The war cry of the MEST universe is: "Must have gotten it somewhere" and "It must have gone somewhere." It will not tolerate the vaguest possibility that one *created* himself, or could *destroy* anything himself.

The whole Sub-zero Scale is a manifestation of one's efforts to combat this demandingness on the part of the MEST universe. Hiding, Protecting, Owning are all mechanisms to answer the questions, "Where did you get it?" "What did you do with it?" The MEST universe, in this light, is essentially a police universe. For it operates upon force and intolerance and demands with pain that its laws be accepted. In that its laws are based solely upon agreement, it is only necessary to discover how to disagree with them to abolish them (or what has been called "natural law for oneself"). Upon the abolishment of this agreement depends the health, progress and advancement of the thetan. This universe is a major expanding trap of finite dimensions and rather idiotic simplicity. If one were to leave the MEST universe, one would solely create space of his own and maintain enough knowledge of what could happen with regard to the MEST universe to defeat its encroachment and its salesmen.

No universe, no matter how cunningly constructed, is entirely proof against this expanding trap. The MEST universe is a game which has gone on too long and of which even the players are tired. Earth could be considered to be, at this time, an egress terminal.

It is noteworthy that one must not accept or know any of these conditions to have these processes work. They act very swiftly and uniformly on any Homo sapiens and upon other beings. A considerable number of the principles which have been discovered in Scientology exist above the MEST universe. The MEST universe, itself, might be considered to be the "inevitable average" of illusion once it starts in a certain direction. We have in natural law, as applied to the MEST universe, the sum of "agreement upon illusion." Tracing the principles of Scientology, as they apply specifically to the MEST universe, is the tracing of the agreements that brought about the MEST universe.

The Axioms of 1951 are, in the main, a tracement of this agreement. The inevitability and "diabolical accuracy" of these predictions of human behavior depend upon their being held in common by Man, which they are. They extend as well to other beings below the level of "player" in this universe and have applied to many sets of players.

While much of the data which has been recovered in this investigation seems, to the narrow scope of Homo sapiens, quite wild—the wildness depends on the absence of investigation in the past and can be compared only to the stupidity which remained ignorant of them. For these matters were an unseen and insidious causation underlying the grief of Earth, at best a pawn in a minor game in a minor galaxy.

∞

Part Three

Standard Operating Procedure 3: Theta Clearing

"Willingness and
unwillingness
to locate things
in time and space
are the key relative
states of sanity."

∞

Chapter Twenty-Seven

STANDARD OPERATING PROCEDURE, ISSUE 3

*"Knowingness
depends upon
certainty."*

STANDARD OPERATING PROCEDURE, ISSUE 3

STANDARD OPERATING PROCEDURE for *Theta Clearing* is the backbone of processing in Scientology. It is easily applied, but the auditor should have an excellent command of all types of processing in order to use it more successfully.

SOP is most easily applied and most successfully by an auditor who is a Theta Clear. Auditors who are not Theta Clear seldom understand it. And a low-toned uncleared auditor, who cannot himself leave the body, very often acts to pin a preclear inside his body. It is noteworthy that many auditors have been unable to obtain success with Theta Clearing before they themselves have been cleared. But immediately after the auditor was cleared, he was successful with each successive case without exception. The fear of some thetans (from various causes) of leaving the body, causes the auditor (who is a thetan) to make other thetans stay in bodies. And it is actually quite dangerous to be audited by auditors who are not Theta Clears. The process is not dangerous…unclear auditors are.

Definitions

THETAN:

This term designates the beingness of the individual, the awareness of awareness unit, that quantity and identity which *is* the preclear. One does not speak of "my thetan" any more than he would speak of "my me." Persons referring to the thetan in such a way as to make the thetan a third party to the body and the person are not only incorrect, they betoken by this a bad state of aberration.

AUDITOR:

The person who "audits," who computes and listens, a practitioner of Dianetics and Scientology. SOP Theta Clearing is best done by an auditor who has been Theta Cleared. A "V" ("five"—see below, under *Standard Operating Procedure*) commonly acts to force the preclear to stay in his body even while pretending to free the preclear from his body.

LOCATION:

The thetan is an energy unit which is located in the center of the skull. It is conceived to be small, but is as large as the preclear believes it to be. A thetan who cannot leave the current body very often believes himself to be holding on *only* to the current body and yet, in actuality, is holding on to a facsimile of an earlier body. The thetan also believes himself to be the size of some earlier body. A thetan from the Fifth Invader Force believes himself to be a very strange insect-like creature with unthinkably horrible hands. He believes himself to be occupying such a body, but is, in actuality, simply a unit capable of producing space, time, energy and matter.

SELF-DETERMINISM:

Self-determinism is a relative state of ability to determine location in time and space, and to create and destroy space, time, energy and matter. If one can locate his facsimiles and ridges in time and space, if one is able to place persons and objects in the past, present and future in time and space, he can be considered to have high self-determinism. If one's facsimiles place him in time and space, if people can easily place one in time and space in the past, present or future, one's self-determinism is low. Willingness and unwillingness to locate things in time and space are the key relative states of sanity.

ILLUSION:

Any idea, space, energy, object or time concept which one creates himself.

REALITY:

That agreement upon illusion which became the MEST universe.

DELUSION:

Things not of one's own creation or of the MEST universe which locate one in time and space.

CERTAINTY:

One is certain on a plus or minus basis and one can be equally certain on either. One can be certain a thing is *not* real or he can be equally certain that it *is* real. There are three sides to this: One is certain a thing is his *own illusion* (this is the highest level). One is certain that a thing is a *MEST universe reality* (illusion). One can be certain that a thing is a *delusion*. Any certainty is a knowingness. Knowingness is sanity. Thus we have three routes of certainty by which to approach knowingness.

KNOWINGNESS:

Knowingness depends upon certainty.

ABERRATION:

Aberration depends upon uncertainty.

THETA PERCEPTION:

That which one perceives by radiating toward an object and from the reflection perceiving various characteristics of the object, such as size, odor, tactile, sound, color, etc. Theta perception is increased by drilling in certainties as above. Theta perception is dependent upon willingness to handle energy and to create space, energy and objects. In view of the fact that the MEST universe can be established easily to be an illusion, one must have an ability to perceive illusions before one can clearly perceive the MEST universe. The thetan who cannot perceive the MEST universe easily will also be found to be incapable of handling and orienting other kinds of illusions with certainty. Theta perception is also a direct index to responsibility, for responsibility is the willingness to handle force.

MEST PERCEPTION:

Recordings the thetan takes from the perception organs of the human body as a shortcut to perception (lazy perception). The body records actual wave emanations from the MEST universe, the thetan uses these recordings. Considerably more data could be collected on this subject.

ORIENTATION:

Determination of location in space and time and determination of energy quantity present. This applies to past, present and future.

RIDGES:

"Solid" accumulations of energy which are suspended in space and time. Ridges can be handled variously. They can also explode.

FACSIMILES:

Energy reproductions of things in the various universes. They are fixed to ridges.

Chapter Twenty-Seven
Standard Operating Procedure, Issue 3

END OF TERMINAL:

A communication line to anything has the preclear at one end and something at the other end. When the end of the terminal is vacated, the flow dams and the preclear must fix the vacated end to his own body. This is the mechanics behind the loss which brings about grief. ARC lines can be mocked-up and handled in the routine of Creative Processing, which process will resolve end of terminal difficulties. These terminals are quite visible to the thetan, who sees them either wound around the body or extending to other bodies or reaching a considerable distance into space. The thetan can actually yank on these terminals, even those which go into space, and free the other end, whether he perceives so or not, and so recover and dispose of such lines.

ASTRAL BODIES:

Somebody's delusion. Astral bodies are usually mock-ups which the mystic then tries to believe real. He sees the astral body as something else and then seeks to inhabit it, in the most common practices of "astral walking." Anyone who confuses astral bodies with thetans is apt to have difficulty with Theta Clearing, for the two things are not the same order of similarity. The exteriorization of a thetan, when actually accomplished, is so complete and thorough and is attended by so many other phenomena that anyone who has made an effort to relate these two things is quite certain to recant after he has been Theta Cleared. The most noteworthy difference is that the thetan does not have a body. Production of illusion to which he then sought to assign MEST reality is probably the underlying factor which makes mysticism so aberrative. Data from India is knowingly or unknowingly "booby-trapped," so that while it contains, if unevaluated and isolated, many essential truths, it contains as well directions which are certain to send the experimenter even more deeply into the unwanted state of becoming MEST. Until recently, the nearest one could come to studying the actuality of existence was through the field of mysticism and its value should not be discounted. But its effect is to deliver an entirely opposite result to any experimenter luckless enough to hope to reach *cause* by becoming an *effect,* as required in mysticism. Seeing and feeling "non-existences" is frightening and harmful only when one seeks to believe them to be existences. Only when he knows he has created them can he obtain a certainty upon them. One can create hallucination for himself only by insisting that what he has created was otherwise created — in short, refusing to accept responsibility for his own created illusions.

ELECTRONICS:

Lower and cruder manifestations of the same order of actuality as thought.

TERMINALS:

In facsimiles, ridges and electric motors, terminals operate and current flows only when they are fixed in time and space. Alternating current becomes possible only because of an overlooked item — the base of the motor — which is fixed in time and space and which keeps the terminals apart by fixing them in time and space.

THE HUMAN SOUL:

The preclear.

MYSTICISM:

Many right ideas but the wrong way to go about it.

FREEDOM:

Ability to create and position energy or matter in time and space.

SLAVERY:
Being positioned in another's time and space.

THE HUMAN BODY:
A carbon-oxygen engine built of complex electronic ridges around the genetic entity which animates it.

THE HUMAN MIND:
The thetan plus the standard memory banks.

STIMULUS-RESPONSE:
The environment of the thetan activating ridges to make them activate the body.

THE REACTIVE MIND:
The ridge automatic response system.

THE SOMATIC MIND:
The genetic entity plus the brain system of the body.

SCIENTOLOGY:
The science of knowing how to know.

KNOWING HOW TO KNOW:
Being the thetan, clear of the body and its ridges, and able to handle illusion, matter, energy, space and time.

THETA CLEAR:
A being who is reasonably stable outside the body and does not come back into the body simply because the body is hurt. No other condition is necessary.

CLEARED THETA CLEAR:
A thetan who is completely rehabilitated and can do everything a thetan should do, such as move MEST and control others from a distance, or create his own universe.

A THETA EXTERIOR:
A thetan who is clear of his body and knows it but is not yet stable outside.

Standard Operating Procedure

This procedure is done in steps. The auditor, with *every* preclear, makes no other judgment than to begin with Step I. And failing to accomplish that immediately, to go to Step II. If he fails to accomplish this immediately, he goes to Step III and so on. When he is able to accomplish a step, he labels the case as that step number, i.e., "a III." He then begins working with that step. After a few hours' work, he again starts at the top with the preclear, with Step I, and progresses on through. Eventually the preclear becomes a Step I.

Step I: Positive Exteriorization

Ask the preclear to "be three feet back of your head." If he does, ask him to go back further, then up, then down, practicing placement in space and time. Then one asks him to see if there are any items in the body he would like to repair and proceeds to let the preclear repair them according to the preclear's own ideas of how he should do it. Then educate the preclear, by asking him to create and destroy his own illusions, into finally getting a certainty of illusion and from this a certainty of perceiving the real universe with all perceptics. (Note: The realest universe is, of course, one's own illusory universe and should be completely rehabilitated before one attempts to perceive or handle or worry about the MEST universe. Rehabilitated, sonic, visio, etc., of the MEST universe are very clear and very certain. Clear perception in early stages is not a test of being outside. The only test is whether the preclear *knows* he is outside.) Change Postulates (Postulate Processing and Rising Scale Processing). Failing the first line of this step, go to Step II.

Step II: By Orientation

Ask the preclear, still inside, to locate the inside of his forehead. Ask him to put a pressor beam against it and push himself out the back of his head. Supplement this by asking him to reach out through the back of his head and grab the wall with a pulling beam and pull himself out. Ask him to steady himself outside and then, by means of beams, to raise and lower himself while outside and to move to various parts of the room while still outside. Use Creative Processing. By orientation as a thetan, placing himself as a thetan in time and space, he becomes sure of his whereabouts. Have him find and cast off old lines which have their terminals fixed to him. Have him find these lines wherever they are and attach them to radiators and water taps and get the energy to drain out of them. The II will ordinarily have enough lines to cause him to snap back in the head when he releases beams. Failing this, go to Step III.

Step III: Space Processing

In that the MEST universe has forced upon the thetan its spatial dimensions and directions, the thetan is likely to become a point which is being subjected to all the counter-efforts and emotions of his environment—for his entire concept of space is being determined by the MEST universe. Have the thetan, still inside, find his feet in the opposite direction from where the MEST body is located by the MEST universe. Have him turn the feet around. Have him create differences in his body and reverse various limbs and positions according to his viewpoint, each one in disagreement with the MEST universe, particularly as appertains to gravity and other influences.

This sets up an ability to disagree with the MEST universe in terms of space. Have him locate his eyes in the back of his head, on the soles of his feet and in other places. Have him assume other bodies, each time changing them slightly and putting them away. Then have him gather himself into his normal MEST universe spatial area and go to Step I.

Step IV: Ridge Running

Ask the preclear to give himself a command to walk. Let him locate the white flow line which results inside his head. When this line goes dark, have him locate the tiny ridge inside the skull that stopped it. Have him run the flow from this barrier (these barriers, they are tiny ridges and each has a thought with it such as "Can't walk" or "Too bored to walk") back toward the spot where he told himself to walk. It will run white for a moment and then go black. Then have him give himself the command to walk again and "watch" this flow line. It may run through two or three tiny barriers and then stop. Again have him run the "objection" to walking. Have him watch the objection flow until it goes black. Then have him give himself the command to walk again and so on and so on. He will wind up at some outside point. Now have him give himself the command "Listen" and have him run this and its back flows on Black and White until he is exterior on the subject of listen. Then use the command "Talk" similarly. Then the command "Nod," then the command "Move," etc. Give "Look" last, for it may "blind" his perception of black and white. He may, each time, get out to a distance in another quarter. If he can do all this, start with Step I again. Failing this step, failing to "see" black and white energy manifestations, go to Step V.

Step V: Black and White Control Processing

Give the preclear a complete E-Meter assessment, using the principles of what he would Create or Destroy or would not Create or would not Destroy (see *Preclear Assessments: Creation and Destruction*). Use this data to make mock-ups. Then have the preclear create and perceive black spots and then white spots, black crosses and white crosses, and move these here and there through the room or through his own space. Turn them on and off, interchanging them, put them in yesterday, put them in tomorrow, make them get larger, make them get smaller, each time doing as much as the preclear can do. Each time one asks him to perceive one of his own created illusions, in terms of black and white spots or crosses, one attempts to coax him into successful control of it. Audit very persuasively and lightly. This preclear ordinarily is frightened of blackness because it either can contain dangerous things, or contains nothing, and he cannot differentiate which. Thus he cannot control blackness and, in being unable to control blackness, flounders in it. He also has a more basic computation that blackness is the only safe thing in which to hide and, therefore, blackness is a thing to have. Further, blackness "takes" things for him. This preclear may be afraid of the police, may believe himself to have a hideous body, theta-wise, and has many other reasons why he cannot exteriorize. Drills on creating and perceiving black and white should be continued until he can handle each easily. The trouble with this preclear, and preclears lower than this, is that they have agreed too heavily with the MEST universe and must be very cautious in confronting it — since in that direction they conceive to lie a much more complete defeat even than that from which they are now suffering.

Audit him also very heavily on Creative Processing *(Self Analysis in Scientology)*. Then go through steps again. If the preclear is immediately perceived to have little or no reality on *any* incident, go to Step VI.

Step VI: ARC Straightwire

Drill, by direct questioning, on locks until the preclear can remember something really "real" to him, something which he "really loved," something with which he was in communication. Then drill him on creating illusions until he is certain he has created one which really isn't real, which he is certain *he* put the emotion and perception into. (See *Self Analysis in Scientology* with attention to End of Session Processing.) Then go through steps again. Failing Step VI after a quick test, go to Step VII.

Step VII: Present Time Body Orientation

Have preclear locate a part of his body and recognize it as such. Have him locate furniture, fixtures, auditor in room. Have him locate the town and country he is in. Get him to find something in present time, which is really real to him, with which he can communicate. Work on this until he can do this. Then go to Step VI. Then go to Step I.

∞

Preclear Assessments

∞

"...every man is
his own universe
and possesses
within himself
all the capabilities
of a universe."

Chapter Twenty-Eight

BE, DO, HAVE & SPACE, ENERGY, TIME TRIANGLE

"Space, Time and Energy, in experience, become Be, Have and Do..."

Chapter Twenty-Eight

BE, DO, HAVE & SPACE, ENERGY, TIME TRIANGLE

HE PHYSICIST HAS long been on a carousel with regard to the component parts of the material universe. He has had to define time in terms of space and energy, space in terms of time and energy, energy in terms of time and space, and matter as a combination of all three. When three factors exist at such an altitude in a science, there can be no further clarification unless the material can be related to experience of an equal magnitude.

The current definitions in Scientology have this liability: If self-determinism is the location of matter and energy in time and space, and the creation, change and destruction of time and space, then there is no comparable data by which to evaluate this level.

The physicist has found the interrelationship — time, space and energy — to be invaluable, and has indeed produced a civilization from this interrelationship. Just as, with our definition of self-determinism, it is possible to de-aberrate an individual and increase his potentialities in a way never before suspected possible and with a speed which exceeds all past estimations, even in the science of Scientology.

Because we are now working from a higher understanding than time, space and energy, it is possible to compare these to experience in such a way as to broaden their use and modify their force or increase it. Control of time, space and energy comes now well within our capabilities.

Space, Time and *Energy,* in experience, become *Be, Have* and *Do* — the component parts of experience itself.

Space = Be

Space could be said to *be.* One can be in a space without change and without time. And one can also be without action.

Time = Have

The essence of *time* is apparently possession *(have)*. When possession ceases, the record of time ceases. Without possession, change cannot be observed. In the presence of possession, change can be observed. Thus it is deduced that time and possession are interdependent.

The *past* could be sub-divided into "had," "should have had," "did not have" and "got," "should have gotten," "did not get" and "gave," "should have given," "did not give."

The *present* could be sub-divided into "have," "should have," "do not have" and "giving," "should be giving," "not giving" and "receiving," "should be receiving," "not receiving."

The *future* is sub-divided into "will have," "should have," "will not have" and "getting," "will be getting," "will not be getting" and "will receive," "will not receive."

In each of the above (past, present and future) the word would apply for any individual, or any part of the dynamics, to all the other dynamics.

The way one knows there was a past is by knowing the conditions of the past. The most revelatory of these is the facsimile which was taken in the past. However, without any possession in the present stemming forward from the past, the past becomes unimportant. Or because possession ceased, the past is obliterated. The single matter of the body of a past life not being in the present life invalidates the existence of the past life to the individual who then does not, or does not care to, remember it. Yet the facsimiles can nevertheless be effective upon him.

Similarly, the individual does not conceive, to any extent, time past the death of his body — since he will have no body.

Energy, whether in the field of thought, emotion or effort, can be summed into *do.* It requires beingness and havingness in order to achieve doingness. Here we have the static of space acting against the kinetic of possession to produce action in the field of thought, emotion or effort (the various categories of doingness).

Should one care to test this as a process on a preclear, he will find that the missing portions of the preclear's past have to do with loss of something. Loss, itself, is the single most aberrative factor in living. It has long been known in this science that the release of a grief charge was an important single improvement in the preclear. Grief is entirely and only concerned with loss or threatened loss. Pain itself can be defined in terms of loss. For pain is the threat which tells one that loss of mobility, or a portion of the body or the environment, is imminent. Man has pain so thoroughly identified with loss that in some languages the words are synonymous.

Loss is always identified with *have*. For if one doesn't have, one cannot lose.

The Hindu sought to depart into his Nirvana by refusing to have anything to do with having. He sought thus to promote himself into *being*. He saw that as long as he retained a grasp on a body in any degree, he was *having* and thus was pressed into *doing*.

Having and being are often identified to the degree that many people attempt exclusively to *be* only by *having*. The capitalist judges his own beingness solely by the degree of possession, not even vaguely by the degree of action he is able to execute.

Possessions absorb and enforce time. Only without possessions would one be able to regulate time at will. This is a singular attribute of the Cleared Theta Clear. And to him possession of MEST is extremely unimportant.

One can make up for a lack of having by doing. And by doing, accomplishes having and thus regulates time.

Having enhances either being or doing, as is sometimes severely recognized by one who would like to take a vacation or a trip to foreign lands.

Doing can enhance either being or having. A balanced doing slants in both directions. But if one does without having, his being increases, as is well known by anyone who insists on doing favors without recompense and without gain.

There is an optimum speed of doing. If one travels less than that speed, he has little being and having. This is applicable especially to the MEST universe. If one travels greater than that speed, he has to abandon both being and having.

The case of the racing driver is in point. He must assume a contempt for being and having in order to achieve the speeds he does.

When change is too rapid, both beingness and havingness suffer. When change is too slow, both beingness and havingness suffer. For change is essentially the redirection of energy.

In the assessment of a preclear, one can easily trace—by use of the triangle *Be, Have* and *Do,* and by placing this over a second triangle with *Space* at the point of Be, *Time* at the point of Have and *Energy* at the point of Do—where the preclear is overbalanced and why the preclear cannot handle time, or why life is complicated with too much havingness and has reduced his beingness to nought, or why he is trying to occupy too much space without being able to fill it.

In the MEST universe, as well as in a constructed universe, these three factors should be balanced for orderly progress.

∞

∞

Chapter Twenty-Nine

CREATION AND DESTRUCTION

"*Unlimited creation without any destruction would be insane. Unlimited destruction without any creation would be similarly insane.*"

CREATION AND DESTRUCTION

$\mathcal{T}$HE CYCLE OF a universe could be said to be the cycle of *creation, growth, conservation, decay* and *destruction*. This is the cycle of an entire universe or any part of that universe. It is also the cycle of life forms.

This would compare to the three actions of energy, which are *start, change* and *stop,* where creation is start, growth is enforced change, conservation and decay are inhibited change and destruction is stop.

The two extremes of the cycle—*creation* and *destruction,* or in the terms of motion, *start* and *stop* —are interdependent and are consecutive.

There could be no creation without destruction. As one must eradicate the tenement before building the apartment house, so in the material universe must destruction and creation be intermingled. A good action could be said to be one which accomplished the maximal construction with minimal destruction. A bad action could be said to be one which accomplished the minimal construction with maximal destruction.

That which is started and cannot be stopped and that which is stopped without being permitted to run a course are, alike, actions bordering upon the psychotic. Unreasonableness, itself, is defined by persistence in one or the other of these courses of starting something which cannot be stopped (as in the case of an A-bomb) or of stopping something before it has reached a beneficial stage.

Unlimited creation without any destruction would be insane. Unlimited destruction without any creation would be similarly insane.

In actuality, insanity can be grouped and classified, detected and remedied, by a study of creation and destruction.

An individual will not be responsible for that on which he will not use force. The definition of responsibility is entirely within this boundary. That person will not be responsible in that sphere where he cannot tolerate force. And if one discovers in an individual where he will not use force, he will find where that individual will also refuse to be responsible.

An assessment of a case can be done by use of the accompanying graph. We see here Creation, with an arrow pointing straight downward, and find there the word Insane. And under this we list the dynamics. Wherever along any of these dynamics the individual cannot conceive himself to be able to create, on that level he will be found aberrated to the degree that he does not believe himself able to create. This might be thought to introduce an imponderable, but such is not the case. For the individual is most aberrated on the First Dynamic and, rightly or wrongly, conceives that he could not create himself. This goes to the extent, in Homo sapiens, of believing that one cannot create a body and, rightly or wrongly, one is then most aberrated on the subject of his body.

Potentially, because of the character of theta itself, an individual in an absolute and possibly unattainable state should be able to create a universe. Certainly it is true that every man is his own universe and possesses within himself all the capabilities of a universe.

To the extreme right of the graph, we have the word Destruction and an arrow pointing downward toward Insane. And beneath this, the list of the dynamics. That individual who can only destroy along any of these dynamics, and cannot or will not create, could be said to be aberrated on that dynamic. He is aberrated to the degree that he would destroy that dynamic.

CREATION		DESTRUCTION	
INSANE	SANE		INSANE
CREATE	GROW CONSERVE DECAY		DESTROY
Start	Change		Stop
Differentiate	Associate		Identify
Be	Do		Have
Space	Energy		Time
40.0	20.0		0.0
Dynamic 1	Dynamic 1		Dynamic 1
Dynamic 2	Dynamic 2		Dynamic 2
Dynamic 3	Dynamic 3		Dynamic 3
Dynamic 4	Dynamic 4		Dynamic 4
Dynamic 5	Dynamic 5		Dynamic 5
Dynamic 6	Dynamic 6		Dynamic 6
Dynamic 7	Dynamic 7		Dynamic 7
Dynamic 8	Dynamic 8		Dynamic 8

Looking again at the column of Creation, one finds the individual aberrated anywhere along the dynamics in that column where the individual will only create and will not destroy.

In the Destruction column, one finds the individual aberrated on any dynamic in that column where he will only destroy.

In the middle ground of the graph, we find that a balance of Creation and Destruction is Sane. And in the dynamics below it, we find the individual sane wherever he will create and destroy.

Use of this graph and these principles enable the auditor to assess hitherto hidden compulsions and obsessions on the part of the preclear.

This is an auditing graph. If one looks at it in another way than auditing, he finds there laid out what has occasionally been posed as a philosophy of existence. Friedrich Nietzsche, in his book *Thus Spake Zarathustra,* presents as a desirable code of conduct, "unlimited willingness to destroy." Philosophically, the code has little or no workability. In order to survive in any universe, conduct must be regulated by a sense of ethics. Ethics are possible on a reasonable level only when the individual is high on the Tone Scale. In the absence of such height, ethics are supplanted by morals, which can be defined as "an arbitrary code of conduct not necessarily related to reason." Should one attempt to regulate his conduct on the basis of unlimited creation or destruction, he would find it necessary to act entirely without judgment to put his philosophy into effect. It is noteworthy that the late Nazi regime can serve as a clinical test of the workability of a scheme of things wherein unlimited creation and destruction are held as an ideal. I heard a rumor lately that Adolf Hitler was dead.

∞

"*A thetan can be*

∞

Book Two

1953

what he can see. He can see what he can be."

∞

Part One

The Factors

"The first action of beingness is to assume a viewpoint."

Chapter One

The Factors

"And thus there is life."

$\mathcal{T}$HE FACTORS

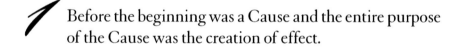

$\mathcal{S}$ummation of the considerations and examinations of the human spirit and the material universe completed between 1923 and 1953 A.D.)

1 Before the beginning was a Cause and the entire purpose of the Cause was the creation of effect.

2 In the beginning and forever is the decision and the decision is TO BE.

3 The first action of beingness is to assume a viewpoint.

4 The second action of beingness is to extend from the viewpoint, points to view, which are dimension points.

5 Thus there is space created, for the definition of space is: viewpoint of dimension. And the purpose of a dimension point is space and a point to view.

6 The action of a dimension point is reaching and withdrawing.

7 And from the viewpoint to the dimension points there are connection and interchange: thus new dimension points are made: thus there is communication.

8 And thus there is LIGHT.

9 And thus there is energy.

10 And thus there is life.

11 But there are other viewpoints and these viewpoints outthrust points to view. And there comes about an interchange amongst viewpoints; but the interchange is never otherwise than in terms of exchanging dimension points.

12 The dimension point can be moved by the viewpoint, for the viewpoint, in addition to creative ability and consideration, possesses volition and potential independence of action: and the viewpoint, viewing dimension points, can change in relation to its own or other dimension points or viewpoints and thus comes about all the fundamentals there are to motion.

13 The dimension points are each and every one, whether large or small, *solid*. And they are solid solely because the viewpoints say they are solid.

14 Many dimension points combine into larger gases, fluids or solids: thus there is matter. But the most valued point is admiration, and admiration is so strong its absence alone permits persistence.

15 The dimension point can be different from other dimension points and thus can possess an individual quality. And many dimension points can possess a similar quality and others can possess a similar quality unto themselves. Thus comes about the quality of classes of matter.

16 The viewpoint can combine dimension points into forms and the forms can be simple or complex and can be at different distances from the viewpoint and so there can be combinations of form. And the forms are capable of motion and the viewpoints are capable of motion and so there can be motion of forms.

17 And the opinion of the viewpoint regulates the consideration of the forms, their stillness or their motion, and these considerations consist of assignment of beauty or ugliness to the forms and these considerations alone are art.

18 It is the opinions of the viewpoints that some of these forms should endure. Thus there is survival.

19 And the viewpoint can never perish; but the form can perish.

20 And the many viewpoints, interacting, become dependent upon one another's forms and do not choose to distinguish completely the ownership of dimension points and so comes about a dependency upon the dimension points and upon the other viewpoints.

21 From this comes a consistency of viewpoint of the interaction of dimension points and this, regulated, is TIME.

22 And there are universes.

23 The universes, then, are three in number: the universe created by one viewpoint, the universe created by every other viewpoint, the universe created by the mutual action of viewpoints which is agreed to be upheld—the physical universe.

24 And the viewpoints are never seen. And the viewpoints consider more and more that the dimension points are valuable. And the viewpoints try to become the anchor points and forget that they can create more points and space and forms. Thus comes about scarcity. And the dimension points can perish and so the viewpoints assume that they, too, can perish.

25 Thus comes about death.

26 The manifestations of pleasure and pain, of thought, emotion and effort, of thinking, of sensation, of affinity, reality, communication, of behavior and being are thus derived and the riddles of our universe are apparently contained and answered herein.

27 There *is* beingness, but Man believes there is only becomingness.

28 The resolution of any problem posed hereby is the establishment of viewpoints and dimension points, the betterment of condition and concourse amongst dimension points and, thereby, viewpoints, and the remedy of abundance or scarcity in all things, pleasant or ugly, by the rehabilitation of the ability of the viewpoint to assume points of view and create and uncreate, neglect, start, change and stop dimension points of any kind at the determinism of the viewpoint. Certainty in all three universes must be regained, for certainty, not data, is knowledge.

29 In the opinion of the viewpoint, any beingness, any thing, is better than no thing, any effect is better than no effect, any universe better than no universe, any particle better than no particle, but the particle of admiration is best of all.

30 And above these things there might be speculation only. And below these things there is the playing of the game. But these things which are written here Man can experience and know. And some may care to teach these things and some may care to use them to assist those in distress and some may desire to employ them to make individuals and organizations more able and so could give to Earth a culture of which Earth could be proud.

Humbly tendered as a gift to Man
by L. Ron Hubbard
April 23, 1953

Chapter Two

VIEWPOINTS & DIMENSION POINTS

"Space is the viewpoint of dimension."

Chapter Two

VIEWPOINTS &
DIMENSION POINTS

Space

THE WORKABLE definition of space is "viewpoint of dimension." There is no space without viewpoint. There is no space without points to view.

This definition of space supplies a very great lack in the field of physics, which defines space simply as "that thing in which energy acts." Physics has defined space as change of motion or in terms of time and energy. Time has been defined in terms of space and energy. Energy has been defined in terms of space and time only. These definitions, thus interdependent, made a circle out of which there was no exit unless one had a better definition for one of those items—time, space or energy. In such a way was the science of physics limited.

Space is the *viewpoint of dimension*. The position of the viewpoint can change. The position of the dimension points can change.

A *dimension point* is any point in a space or at the boundaries of space. As a specialized case, those points which demark the outermost boundaries of the space or its corners are called, in Scientology, *anchor points*. An anchor point is a specialized kind of dimension point.

Any energy has, as its basic particle, a dimension point. The dimension point can be of different kinds and substances. It can combine in various ways, it can take on forms, become objects, it can flow as energy. A particle of admiration or a particle of force are, alike, dimension points.

Dimension points, by shifting, can give the viewpoint the illusion of motion. The viewpoint, by shifting, can give the dimension points the illusion of motion. Motion is the manifestation of change of viewpoint of dimension points.

Viewpoints are not visible, but viewpoints can have dimension points which are themselves visible. The basic hidden influence is, then, a viewpoint. A material of the universe cannot exist in any universe without something in which to exist. The something in which it exists is space. And this is made by the attitude of a viewpoint which demarks an area with anchor points.

Rather than existing on theory, in common with other principles of Scientology, this manifestation of created space can be experienced by an individual who discovers that space can be made coincidentally with any other space.

Space, then, is not an arbitrary and absolute, but is creatable or uncreatable by a viewpoint.

Any being is a viewpoint. He is as much a being as he is able to assume viewpoints. Thus in any society we would inevitably have a statement of the infinity of viewpoint, such as "God is everywhere." Beings instinctively assign the most beingness to that thing which would be everywhere. And when Man desires to assign an unlimited power or command to anything, he says that it is everywhere.

Beingness

In this universe, in order to achieve a state of beingness it is necessary to have a viewpoint from which dimension points can be created or controlled. One has as much viewpoint as he has space in which to view, in relationship to other viewpoints having space in which to view. Thus one has a condition of relative beingness.

Energy

The basic unit of energy is the dimension point. A specialized kind of dimension point is the anchor point which demarks space. But this is again the basic unit of energy. Dimension points are created, controlled or uncreated by the thetan.

Matter

In order to have space, it is necessary to have a viewpoint and the potential in the viewpoint of creating anchor points. Thus in order to view matter, much less control or create it, it is necessary to have a viewpoint.

∞

Chapter Three

𝒰NIVERSES

"*A universe
is defined as
a 'whole system
of created things.'*"

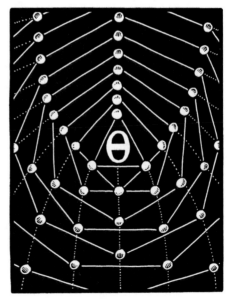

Chapter Three

UNIVERSES

A UNIVERSE IS DEFINED as a "whole system of created things." There could be and are many universes and there could be many kinds of universes.

We are, for our purposes here, interested in two particular universes. The first of these is the *MEST universe,* that agreed-upon reality of matter, energy, space and time which we use as anchor points and through which we communicate. The other is our *personal universe,* which is no less a matter of energy and space. These two universes are entirely distinct and it could be said that the principal confusion and aberration of the individual stems from his having confused one for the other. Where these two universes have crossed in the mind of the individual, we find a confusion of control and ownership for the reason that the two universes do not behave alike.

Whereas each one of these universes was apparently founded on the same modus operandi as any other universe (which is to say, the creation of space by putting out anchor points, the formation of forms by combinations of dimension points), the MEST universe and one's own universe do not behave similarly *for him.*

One's own universe is amenable to instantaneous creation and destruction, by himself and without argument. He can create space and bring it into a "permanent status." He can create and combine forms in that space and cause those forms to go into motion. And he can make that motion continuously automatic, or he can regulate it sporadically, or he can regulate it totally, and all by postulate. One's envisionment of one's own universe is intensely clear. The reality of one's own universe is sharper and brighter, if anything, than his reality on the MEST universe.

We call one's attitude toward his own universe "actuality" and his attitude toward the MEST universe, since it is based upon agreement, "reality."

Unless an individual is at a very high operating level, he conceives it necessary to use physical force and to apply MEST universe forces to MEST universe forces in order to get action, motion and new forms. His activity in the MEST universe is an activity of handling energy and his ability to exist in the MEST universe is conditional upon his ability to use force. The MEST universe is essentially a force universe — a fact which is, incidentally, antipathetic to most thetans. One's ability to handle the MEST universe is conditional upon his not abdicating from his right to use force, right to give orders, his right to punish, his right to administer personal justice and so forth. We are presented in the MEST universe with a crude and brutal scene, wherein gigantic forces are in pressure against gigantic forces and where the end of all seems but destruction. Paradoxically, in the MEST universe, destruction of form only is possible since, by the law of the "conservation of energy," the destruction of actual material objects is impossible — only conversion being attainable.

In the MEST universe, ethics seem to be a liability. Honesty is all but impossible, save when armed with force of vast magnitude. Only the strong can afford to be ethical. And yet the use of strength begets but the use of strength. In the MEST universe we are confronted with paradoxes upon paradoxes where behavior is concerned, for behavior in the MEST universe is regulated by stimulus-response and not by analytical thought or reason. The MEST universe demands of us complete and utter obedience and agreement on the penalty of extermination. Yet when one has agreed entirely with the MEST universe, he finds himself unable to perceive it with clarity.

In one's own universe, on the other hand, honesty, ethics, happiness, good behavior, justice all become possible.

It is one of the operations of the MEST universe that it is a jealous universe. And those who are thoroughly imbued with the principles of the MEST universe have, even at their best efforts, the goal of eradicating one's own universe. A control operation begins early in the life of almost every man, whereby his imagination is condemned. His own universe is not imaginary, but it may be said to be so. And if his imagination is condemned, then he loses his ability to garnish the hardness and brutality of the MEST universe with hopes and dreams. When he loses this, he becomes a slave of the MEST universe. And as a slave, he perishes. His road to immortality lies, then, in another direction than in the complete subservient agreement with the MEST universe and the handling and conversion of its forces. This is a matter which has been subjected continuously to test. And it is intensely surprising to people to discover that the rehabilitation of their creative ability, their own space, their own images, rehabilitates as well their ability to confront the MEST universe with a strong and ethical face.

Creative Processing (especially where it divorces all thought from thought of the MEST universe and follows out along a line of the rehabilitation of one's own universe without attention to the MEST universe) is one level of processing which produces magnificent results and which is a standby in any case, no matter how difficult.

On the other hand, the rehabilitation of the MEST universe itself, in the concept of the individual, accomplishes a very great deal in processing and could be said to compare with the rehabilitation of one's own universe. But the rehabilitation of one's ability to perceive the MEST universe is dependent upon his ability to perceive present time and the rehabilitation of that ability. Dwelling with the MEST universe past or its future is fruitless. Thinking about the MEST universe, attempting to predict the MEST universe, planning to reorganize and handle the MEST universe all defeat one's ability to handle the MEST universe. When he simply begins to perceive the MEST universe in present time and to examine that which he sees, with the idea that he can be what he sees, he loses all fear of the MEST universe.

There is a differentiation process in one's own universe, a differentiation process exclusively for the MEST universe and a differentiation process which pulls apart one's own universe and the MEST universe. The first of these processes simply goes about reconstructing one's own universe with no attention to the MEST universe. The second causes the individual to contact the MEST universe present time and to observe that present time continuously. The third differentiates between the MEST universe and one's own universe and consists of mocking-up one's own universe duplicate of every MEST universe object he can perceive, and then actually comparing these one against the other (this process is called *Duplicating*).

Creating space and mocking-up items in it is the rehabilitation of one's own universe and is a primary process.

Differentiating between two similar objects in the MEST universe (such as two books, two chairs, two spaces) with one's MEST eyesight, accomplishes much in being able to face and handle the MEST universe.

The mocking-up of MEST universe duplicates (which is to say, constructing a universe parallel to the MEST universe) is the mechanism by which facsimiles are made and this process brings under control the mechanisms which make facsimiles.

The original definition of Scientology 8-8008 was the attainment of infinity (8) by the reduction of the apparent infinity (8) and power of the MEST universe to a zero (0) for himself, and the increase of the apparent zero (0) of one's own universe to an infinity (8) for oneself. This is an ideal and theoretical process. It is not necessarily attainable in actuality or reality, but it very well may be. It can be seen that infinity stood upright makes the number eight. Thus, Scientology 8-8008 is not just another number, but serves to fix into the mind of the individual a route by which he can rehabilitate himself, his abilities, his ethics and his goals.

∞

Chapter Four

BEHAVIOR OF UNIVERSES

"The MEST universe is that upon which one agrees in order to continue in association with other viewpoints."

Chapter Four

$\mathcal{B}$EHAVIOR OF UNIVERSES

T COULD BE SAID, then, that the difference between the microcosm (one's own universe) and the macrocosm (the MEST universe) is the difference between *commanding* it and *agreeing* about it.

One's own universe is what he would construct for a universe without the opposition or the confusion of other viewpoints. The MEST universe is that upon which one agrees in order to continue in association with other viewpoints. This may very well be the sole difference between these two universes.

This is exemplified by one's behavior-attitude in his own universe as compared with his behavior-attitude in the MEST universe. In one's own universe, the individual expansively plans and devises (once he is fairly confident of it) along the lines of beauty and happiness. In the MEST universe, even when one has been rehabilitated to some degree, one's attitude still must consist of a certain amount of watchfulness and cooperation.

One's universe is an unthwarted sway. The MEST universe is a compromise. When one has compromised too long and too often, when he has been betrayed and ridiculed and is no longer able to create what he believes to be desirable, he descends down to lower levels. And in those levels, he is still more compelled to face the MEST universe and, as such, loses much more of his ability to handle the MEST universe. When an individual's ability to create his own universe is rehabilitated, it will be found, strangely enough, that his ability to handle the MEST universe has been rehabilitated. In fact, this is the most secure route as represented in 8-8008 as a road.

By actual experiment, it can be demonstrated that one's ability to mock-up a universe of his own, and the resulting improvement of his perceptions to that universe, bring about an ability to perceive the MEST universe. Indeed, it might be inferred as something like a proof that the MEST universe in itself is an illusion based upon agreement, in view of the fact that the rehabilitation of the ability to view illusion rehabilitates the ability to view the MEST universe.

Chapter Five

$\mathscr{T}$ERMINALS

*"At every turn
in the examination
of the MEST universe,
we discover that it is
a two-terminal
universe."*

Chapter Five

TERMINALS

AT EVERY TURN in the examination of the MEST universe, we discover that it is a *two-terminal universe.*

In the manufacture of electricity, it is necessary to have two terminals. In order to have an opinion evaluated, it is necessary to have an opinion against which the first can be evaluated. A datum can be understood in the MEST universe only when it is compared to a datum of comparable magnitude. This is two terminals operating in terms of thought. Two MEST universe terminals which are similar, placed side by side, will discharge to some degree against each other. This is observable in gravity as well as in electricity.

A primary difference between the MEST universe and one's own universe is that one's own universe is not necessarily a two-terminal universe. One can mock-up in one's own universe two terminals which will discharge against each other. But one can also at will mock-up two terminals which are identical, which will not discharge against each other.

There are a number of processes which could include double terminals. One terminal made to face another terminal, in terms of mock-up, can be discharged one against the other in such a way as to relieve aberration connected with things similar to the terminal thus mocked-up.

However, these two terminals do not furnish a double terminal of a communication line. A communication line is more important than a communication point. Thus if one wished to discharge anything, he would desire to discharge the communication line. The MEST universe is intensely dependent upon communication lines rather than communication terminals. One takes two pairs of such terminals, then, and standing them in relationship to each other discovers that he now has four terminals. But these four terminals furnish only two lines. These two lines will discharge one against the other.

This, as a limited process, should not be continued very long. It is of greatest interest in rendering assistance after an accident, where it is only necessary to mock-up the accident twice or, indeed, to mock-up something similar to an injured limb, to have the pain and discomfort and aberration discharged.

Should one burn one's finger, it is necessary only to mock-up his finger twice side by side and then twice again, making four mock-ups with two communication lines, to have the pain in the finger subside. The mock-ups discharge at the same time as one's injured finger re-experiences the incident.

This manifestation is the manifestation of the MEST universe. It is not a manifestation of one's own universe and if practiced over a long period of time is essentially an agreement with the MEST universe — a thing which should be avoided. Thus, it is a limited process.

CHAPTER FIVE
TERMINALS

A terminal is in essence any point of no form, or any form or dimension, from which energy can flow or by which energy can be received. A viewpoint, then, is a sort of terminal. But a terminal must have a particle in order to do automatic interchanges. And one finds that a viewpoint can be affected by the MEST universe only when the viewpoint has identified itself with some MEST universe article, such as a body. The rehabilitation of the viewpoint's ability to *be* or *not be,* at will, is essential in order that a viewpoint be self-determined about what is affecting him and what is not affecting him. This depends then, of course, upon what a viewpoint identifies himself with and depends upon the ability of the viewpoint to unidentify himself rapidly.

Terminals are anywhere in the MEST universe and can be manufactured, of course, in one's own universe. The difference is that any bit of solid (even on the level of an electron) in the MEST universe is, willy-nilly, a terminal. It is affected in certain ways, whether it likes it or not. Any particle in any object or any flow of energy is, in itself, a terminal. A terminal can be affected by any other terminal or can affect, to some degree, other terminals.

This cross-relationship of terminals in the MEST universe is MEST universe communication. In one's own universe a flow is not necessary for the production of energy or potentials.

It is one of the sources of aberration that the scarcity of things in the MEST universe causes one to own only *one* of things. This is aberrative since *one* can gather into itself charges which are not discharged, since there is nothing immediately similar to it. If one owned *two* of everything he had, and if these two things were nearly identical, he would find that his worry and concern about these objects was greatly decreased. A child, for instance, should have two dolls alike, not simply one doll.

The reason for this is that two terminals will discharge, one against the other. The thetan is capable of mocking himself up to be exactly like everything he sees. As a matter of fact, whatever a thetan can see he can be. Thus, the thetan makes himself into a terminal for every terminal he sees whenever there is an absence of a duplicate. Thus, the thetan is in the danger of having everything in the MEST universe discharging against him the moment he alters his relationship to the MEST universe. This fixes him in the belief that he cannot alter his relationship to the MEST universe. Actually, he is rather rapidly disabused of this conception by processing. It is rather interesting to Double Terminal, in mock-up form, the childhood toys of an individual. He will find there is an enormous amount of charge simply in the fact that these toys were made out of MEST. The favorite doll has a gravitic influence upon him.

Completely aside from the terminals one finds in an electric motor (and which produce so much current by reason of being separated by the base of the motor), the subject of terminals goes into behavior and explains, in a great measure, behavior on a stimulus-response basis in the MEST universe. Indeed, it could be said that the MEST universe came into being by one terminal demanding attention from another terminal and these two terminals, thereafter facing each other, continuing a discharge one to the other. With very aberrated people, one cannot long discuss things with them without getting the manifestation of terminals, for the very aberrated people fix on a terminal easily.

It could be said that the MEST universe is the average of agreement amongst viewpoints and that the laws of the MEST universe, no matter how physical, are the result of this agreement. And, indeed, this definition suffices for those conditions which are supposed to be "reality."

The MEST universe is very real. But any hypnotist can instruct a hypnotized subject into the construction of a universe which has tactile, sight, sound and any other manifestation possessed by the MEST universe. And who is to say, then, that the hypnotized subject is not perceiving a universe? For one's own perception of the MEST universe consists of his placing an object in proximity to or against another object and both of these objects are found to be objects of the MEST universe. This is overlooked by individuals when they, for instance, strike a desk with their fist. It is the favorite declaration of the materialist (that individual who is in a frantic state of insistence upon the existence of the MEST universe) that "this is real." The effects he is creating are being created by a hand that is made out of MEST on an object which is MEST. The individual has overlooked the fact that the hand with which he is doing the pounding is itself MEST and that his knowledge of that hand is actually no more than his perception of it. This is a problem in two terminals.

∞

Chapter Six

$\mathcal{L}$OGIC

*"Logic is
the combination
of factors into
an answer."*

$\mathcal{L}$OGIC

OGIC IS a gradient scale of association of facts, of greater or lesser similarity, made to resolve some problem of the past, present or future, but mainly to resolve and predict the future.

Logic is the combination of factors into an answer. The mission of the analytical mind, when it thinks, is to observe and predict by the observation of results. Easily the best way to do this is to be the objects one is observing, thus one can *know* their condition completely. However, if one is not sufficiently up the scale to be these objects, it is necessary to *assume* what they are. This assumption of what they are, the postulating of a symbol to represent the objects, and the combination of these symbols when evaluated against past experience or "known law," bring about logic.

The genesis of logic may be said to be an interchange of two viewpoints, via other dimension points, by which one of the viewpoints holds the attention (one of the most valuable commodities in the universe) of the other viewpoint by being "logical" about why that viewpoint should continue to look.

The basis of logic is "it is bad over there" or "there is a hidden influence, which you cannot estimate, but which we will try to estimate," "therefore, you should continue to look toward me."

At its best, logic is rationalization. For all logic is based upon the somewhat idiotic circumstance that a being that is immortal is trying to survive. Survival is a condition susceptible to non-survival. If one is "surviving," one is at the same moment admitting that one can cease to survive. Otherwise, one would never strive to survive. An immortal being striving to survive presents immediately a paradox. An immortal being must be persuaded that he cannot survive, or that he is not and might become nought, before he would pay any attention to logic. By logic, he can then estimate the future. Probably the only reason he would want to estimate the MEST universe, aside from amusement, is to keep alive in it or to maintain something in a state of life in it. Logic and survival are intimate. But it must be remembered that if one is worried about his own survival and is striving for his own survival, he is striving for the survival of an immortal being. Bodies are transient, but bodies are an illusion. One could bring himself up the Tone Scale to a point where he could create an imperishable body with ease.

It is interesting that those people who are the most logical are those people who in processing have to *know* before they *are*. When they are sent somewhere, they want to know what is there before they get there. There would be no point in going there if they knew and if everyone knew what was there before they went there. Yet they will attempt to predict what is going to happen there and what is there by knowing. This knowingness is in terms of data and should not be confused with knowingness in terms of actual beingness. Logic is the use of data to produce knowingness. As such, it is very junior to knowing something by being it.

CHAPTER SIX
LOGIC

If you were to Double Terminal an individual who is customarily very logical, his body facing his body in terms of mock-up and each of the terminals being very logical, a surprising violence of interchange would take place. This is because logic is mainly aberration.

The work which lies before you is a discussion of beingness and is the track of agreement which became, evidently, the MEST universe. Therefore this work appears to be logical. But it also appears to be the central thread of logic. Apparently these conclusions were reached by logic. They were not. They were reached by observation and by induction. That, when tested, they proved themselves in terms of behavior, demonstrates not that they are logical—but that they are, at least to a large extent, a discussion of beingness. Scientific logic and mathematical logic have the frailty of trying to find out what is there before one goes there. One cannot ever be if he has to know a datum about the beingness first. If one is afraid to be, one will become, of course, logical. This is no effort to be abusive upon the subject of logic or mathematics. It is only necessary at this point to indicate a certain difference between what lies before you and a logical arrangement of assumption.

Chapter Seven

ASSISTS

"*Using effort to control one's mock-ups is of little avail. One simply creates them.*"

Chapter Seven

ASSISTS

S NOTED EARLIER under *Terminals,* an assist can be rendered by mocking-up the injured part or the scene of injury as two terminals and holding or re-creating these mock-ups until the injury abates.

While doing this, it will be noted particularly that the mock-ups are at first uncontrollable (in most cases) and then become much more easily controlled. The uncontrollable factor of the mock-ups is answered by this: Whenever a pair of mock-ups or a single mock-up misbehaves (which is to say, acts without the specific command of the person getting the mock-up), the person doing the mock-up should simply abandon the pair or single mock-up and put into its place, again, one which is doing what he wants it to do. In other words, a disobedient mock-up or pair of mock-ups is either put away or moved to the right or left or forced into control. And in its place the individual simply puts a mock-up which is obedient to his control.

An auditor should be careful on this point. For an individual getting mock-ups will strain and worry and eventually discover, he thinks, that it is impossible for him to control his mock-ups. Using effort to control one's mock-ups is of little avail. One simply creates them. Where mock-ups are absent, one will appear if the individual will simply keep putting the thought forward that it will appear. If he puts forward the thought, often enough and long enough, he will get such a mock-up. Where he can get only one of a pair of mock-ups, if he will keep putting the second one in, it will eventually appear.

What one is facing in Double Terminaling, here, is so much charge on a single subject that the charge dissipates the mock-up before the mock-up can be adequately perceived. No matter how briefly, when an individual has said a mock-up will be there, a mock-up has appeared. That it has disappeared promptly does not mean that he cannot put up a second mock-up there.

Particular attention should be given to this in assists, because an assist is essentially an injured member or a scene which contains *pain*. In Double Terminaling assists, it will be found that the preclear becomes ill or in pain in spite of how innocent he may feel it is to hold two terminals out in front of him. The remedy for this is simply to hold the two terminals, or replace them if they disappear or misbehave, until the illness or feeling has abated.

One can handle worries in this fashion. One simply puts up one worry and then duplicates it, facing itself out in front of him, and the thought discharges against the thought until the worry and the emotion connected with the worry disappear. Thought, emotion and effort can be dissipated by Double Terminaling in this fashion.

It is again remarked that this is a limited technique and should not be continued endlessly as an end in itself. Thirty or forty hours of Double Terminaling is much more than enough. The route pointed out by Scientology 8-8008 is a better route than Double Terminaling. Double Terminaling is relegated to the level of assist and changing one's state of mind. Double Terminaling doubt against doubt undermines and gets at the bottom of every circuit. Thus it, as a technique, should not be entirely neglected.

∞

Chapter Eight

$\mathscr{C}$OMMUNICATION

*"Beingness,
communication, space
are, in action,
synonyms."*

COMMUNICATION

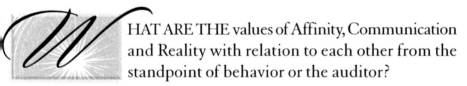

HAT ARE THE values of Affinity, Communication and Reality with relation to each other from the standpoint of behavior or the auditor?

Affinity is *type* of energy and can be produced at will.

Reality is *agreement*. Too much agreement under duress brings about the vanishment of one's entire consciousness.

Communication, however, is *far* more important than affinity or reality. For it is the operation, the *action,* by which one experiences emotion and by which one agrees. Communication is not only the modus operandi, it *is* the heart of life and *is* by thousands of percent the senior in importance to affinity and reality. And this is easily demonstrated, for only if the auditor concentrates on communication can he resolve problems, predict behavior and alter or control minds.

Sharply, then, alert to this value of communication and do not go on trying to make a thirst for love make love all, or a hope for agreement the all. The important answer is found, *always,* in the modus operandi of communication. Communication is at once the strongest hope for resolving any problem of behavior and the weakest commodity in the case one confronts. Fail to observe the singular magnitude of communication, when evaluated against agreement and affinity, and fail with cases. It almost does not matter *what* is communicated if it *is* communicated.

The one test of aberration is communication lag index. How long does it take to get an answer from the preclear? He is as aberrated as he takes time. He *has* in the degree that he handles particles. The *handling* of particles, of motion, *is* communication. Reality is the consideration of particles. Affinity is the opinion about particles and sensation. Consideration is not beingness. Opinion is not beingness. Only communication ranks with beingness.

The only accurate test of whether or not a case is improved is whether or not there is a communication change. By communication change we also mean *perception* change. Perception is all. And any form of communication is known alone by perception.

A thetan can be what he can see. He can see what he can be. If he can't see it as a thetan (not as MEST eyes), he can't be it. If he can't be it, he can't see it.

A viewpoint puts out anchor points. It now has space. How does it know it has anchor points out? Because it can see them. How does it know there are anchor points at all? Only because it can see them. Then how does it know it has space? Because it can perceive. How does it perceive? By knowing. By knowing a datum? No, by being certain. Knowingness is being-certainness.

One is as certain as he can communicate. He can communicate as well as he can *be*.

Further, one is as *responsible* as one can *communicate*. One is not responsible for that with which he cannot communicate. One will fight only that with which he cannot communicate.

How does one communicate? A method of permissible communication is via MEST. One places his ability into hands, eyes, etc., and by sound waves, light particles and others, communicates. He has "put the blame on MEST." Actually, all these particles are his own *immediate* creation by agreed-upon, implicitly believed ritual. His body, even the Sun, is there because he co-believes with many other viewpoints that they are there. He mocks-up the MEST universe continually, as can be tested by comparison of a MEST universe terminal with a mock-up terminal, many times, each time noting the difference. (Duplicating—see earlier text, *Universes*.) The circuit that automatically mocks-up MEST comes to view and under control.

Get an invalid, by whatever means, pleasant or unpleasant, into communication with a withered limb and it will heal. It requires hours, perhaps, of massage (and the massage or sensation must be sufficiently irregular to continue to command his attention) but it will work, not because of faith but because of continuously commanding the invalid to perceive his leg.

There are many levels of communication. The best is self-determined communication by postulate containing no effort. But any is better than none.

The best communication is by the thetan's own creation, despatch and return of dimension points. That which he thus perceives is really real to him and he takes full responsibility for it. He puts out golden clouds of "flitter" in order to so perceive.

Simply by putting out (by postulate) this flitter, the occluded case can, after several times trying, unmask the black facsimile behind which he is hiding. This is direct thetan communication, the best.

Beingness, communication, space are, in action, synonyms. The 0.2 case has no space. Get him to communicate, he has space. He may feel his body and facsimiles are rock hard. Get him to communicate, to waste anchor points in Expanded GITA (following text — *SOP 8*) and be things and he becomes less aberrated, less in pain, less solid.

If a person cannot communicate, if he has a long communication index lag, he has no great beingness, no space. Spacation *(SOP 8)* solves it, imitating beingness solves it, doing routine mock-ups of any kind solves it (for these are anchor points which make space) and any communication betterment process solves it. Even finding present time solves it.

Thus, see the role that communication plays in the game called Existence.

∞

Part Two

Standard Operating Procedure 8: Operating Thetan

"An Operating Thetan must also be able to manufacture particles of admiration and force in abundance."

∞

Chapter Nine

STANDARD OPERATING PROCEDURE 8

"*The goal of this procedure is Operating Thetan, a higher goal than earlier procedures.*"

STANDARD OPERATING PROCEDURE 8

 N USING this operating procedure, the auditor should give every heed to the Auditor's Code. Further, he should audit the preclear in the presence of a third person or another auditor.

This operating procedure is best done by an auditor who has been thoroughly trained in all processes involving the reduction of the past and its incidents. The untrained auditor may encounter manifestations with which only a professional auditor would be familiar.

This operating procedure retains the most workable methods of preceding procedures and, in itself, emphasizes *positive gain* and the present and future, rather than *negative gain* of eradication of the past.

The thetan, exteriorized and rehabilitated, can handle and remedy, by direct address of his own energy to the body and the removal of old energy deposits, all body malfunctions or mental aberrations attacked by older processes. The goal of this procedure is not the rehabilitation of the body, but of the thetan. Rehabilitation of a body incidentally ensues.

The goal of this procedure is *Operating Thetan,* a higher goal than earlier procedures.

The auditor tests the preclear for each step, from Step I on, until he finds a step the preclear can do. The auditor then completes this step and then the next higher step until the thetan is exteriorized. With the thetan exteriorized, the auditor now completes all seven steps regardless of the steps performed before exteriorization. He may complete all these steps and all parts of these steps rapidly. But they must be done to obtain a Theta Clear and they must be done thoroughly to obtain an Operating Thetan.

The techniques involved herein were tested on a wide variety of cases. It is doubtful if any earlier process of any kind in any age has been as thoroughly validated as this operating procedure. However, it works only when used as stated. Disorganized fragments of this material, given other names and emphases, may be found to be harmful. Irresponsible and untrained use of this procedure is not authorized. Capricious or quasi-religious exteriorization of the thetan, for other purposes than the restoration of his ability and self-determinism, should be resisted by any being. *The goal of this process is freedom for the individual to the betterment of the many.*

Step I

Ask preclear to be three feet behind his head. If stable there, have him be in various pleasant places until any feeling of scarcity of viewpoints is resolved. Then have him be in several undesirable places, then several pleasant places. Then have him be in a slightly dangerous place, then in more and more dangerous places until he can sit in the center of the Sun. Be sure to observe a gradient scale of ugliness and dangerousness of places. Do not let the preclear fail. Then do remaining steps with preclear exteriorized.

Step II

Have preclear mock-up own body. If he does this easily and clearly, have him mock-up own body until he slips out of it. When he is exteriorized and knows it thoroughly (the condition of all exteriorization) do Step I. If his mock-up was not clear, go to Step III immediately.

Step III: Spacation

Have preclear close his eyes and find upper corners of the room. Have him sit there, not thinking, refusing to think of anything, interested only in the corners until he is completely exteriorized without strain. Then do a Spacation (constructing own space with eight anchor points and holding it stable without effort) and go to Step I. If preclear was unable to locate corners of the room easily with his eyes closed, go to Step IV.

Step IV: Expanded GITA

(This is an extension of Give and Take Processing.) Test preclear to see if he can get a mock-up he can see, no matter how vague. Then have him *waste, accept under duress, desire* and finally be able to *take or leave alone* each of the items listed below. He does this with mock-ups or ideas. He must do the sequence of waste, etc., in the order given here for each item. He wastes it by having it at remote distances in places where it will do no good, being used or done or observed by something which cannot appreciate it. When he is able to waste it in vast quantities, the auditor then has him accept it in mock-up form until he no longer is antagonistic to having to accept it even when it is unpleasant and great force is applied to make him take it. Then again, with mock-ups, he must be able to bring himself to desire it even in its worst form. Then, by mock-ups of it in its most desirable form, he must come to be able to leave it entirely alone or take it in its worst form without caring. Expanded GITA remedies contra-survival abundance and scarcity. It will be found that before one can accept a very scarce (to him) thing, he has to give it away. A person with a milk allergy must be able to give away, in mock-up, enormous quantities of milk, wasting it, before he can accept any himself. The items in this list are compounded of several years of isolating what factors were more important to minds than others. The list lacks very few of the very important items, if any. Additions to or subtractions from this list should not be attempted. *Viewpoint, work* and *pain* should be heavily and often stressed and given priority. Next in importance are *incidents, looking, sensation, talking* and *knowing.*

Waste, Have Forced Upon, Desire, Be Able to Give or Take, in that order, each of the following (order of items here is random):

Viewpoint, Work, Pain, Incidents, Looking, Sensation, Talking, Knowing, Beauty, Motion, Engrams, Ugliness, Logic, Pictures, Confinement, Money, Parents, Blackness, Police, Light, Explosions, Bodies, Degradation, Male Bodies, Female Bodies, Babies, Children Male, Children Female, Strange and Peculiar Bodies, Dead Bodies, Affinity (Love), Agreement, Beautiful Bodies, People, Attention, Admiration, Force, Energy, Lightning, Unconsciousness, Problems, Antagonism, Reverence, Fear, Objects, Time, Eating Human Bodies, Sound, Grief, Beautiful Sadness, Hidden Influences, Hidden Communications, Doubts, Faces, Dimension Points, Anchor Points, Anger, Apathy,

Ideas, Enthusiasm, Disagreement, Hate, Sex, Eating Parents, Eaten by Parents, Eating Men, Eaten by Men, Eating Women, Eaten by Women, Starts, Spoken Communications, Written Communications, Stillness, Exhaustion, Stopping Motion Women, Stopping Motion Men, Changing Motion Women, Changing Motion Men, Changing Motion Babies, Changing Motion Children, Starting Motion Men, Starting Motion Women, Starting Motion Children, Starting Motion Objects, Starting Motion Self, Omens, Wickedness, Forgiveness, Play, Games, Machinery, Touch, Traffic, Stolen Goods, Stolen Pictures, Homes, Blasphemy, Caves, Medicine, Glass, Mirrors, Pride, Musical Instruments, Dirty Words (written on paper, in air), Space, Wild Animals, Pets, Birds, Air, Water, Food, Milk, Garbage, Gases, Excreta, Rooms, Beds, Punishment, Boredom, Confusion, Soldiers, Executioners, Doctors, Judges, Psychiatrists, Liquor (Alcohol), Drugs, Masturbation, Rewards, Heat, Cold, Forbidden Things, God, the Devil, Spirits, Bacteria, Glory, Dependence, Responsibility, Wrongness, Rightness, Insanity, Sanity, Faith, Christ, Death, Rank (Position), Poverty, Maps, Irresponsibility, Greetings, Farewells, Credit, Loneliness, Jewels, Teeth, Genitalia, Complications, Help, Pretense, Truth, Lies, Assurance, Contempt, Predictability, Unpredictability, Vacuums, White Clouds, Black Clouds, Unattainables, Hidden Things, Worry, Revenge, Textbooks, Kisses, The Past, The Future, The Present, Arms, Stomachs, Bowels, Mouths, Cigarettes, Smoke, Urine, Vomit, Convulsions, Saliva, Flowers, Semen, Blackboards, Fireworks, Toys, Vehicles, Dolls, Audiences, Doors, Walls, Weapons, Blood, Ambitions, Illusions, Betrayal, Ridicule, Hope, Happiness, Mothers, Fathers, Grandparents, Suns, Planets, Moons, Waiting, Silence, Not Knowing, Fac One, Remembering, Forgetting, Auditing, Minds, Fame, Power, Accidents,

Illnesses, Approval, Tiredness, Acting, Drama, Costumes, Sleep, Holding Things Apart, Holding Things Together, Destroying Things, Sending Things Away, Making Things Go Fast, Making Things Appear, Making Things Vanish, Convictions, Stability, Changing People, Silent Men, Silent Women, Silent Children, Symbols of Weakness, Symbols of Force, Disabilities, Education, Languages, Bestiality, Homosexuality, Invisible Bodies, Invisible Acts, Invisible Scenes, Accepting Things Back, Rules, Players, Restimulation, Sexual Restimulation, Space Reduction, Size Reduction, Entertainment, Cheerfulness, Freedom for Others to Talk, Act, Feel Pain, Be Sad, Thetans, Personalities, Cruelty, Organizations, Nothing.

WARNING: Should your preclear become unstable or upset doing this process, take him to Step VI. Then return to this list.

COMMENT: The mind is sufficiently complicated that it can be expected to have computations on almost all the above. Thus there is no single clearing "button" and search for it is at the dictate of a circuit, the mechanism of circuits being to search for something hidden. Thus your preclear may begin to compute and philosophize and seek to find the "button" that will release all this. All this releases all the buttons, so tell him to relax and go on with the process every time he starts to compute.

NOTE: Running the above will bring to the surface, without further attention, the "computation on the case" and the service facsimile. Do not audit these. Run Expanded GITA.

Step V: Present Time Differentiation.
Exteriorization by Scenery

Have preclear, with his body's eyes, study and see the difference between similar real objects such as the two legs of a chair, the spaces between the back, two cigarettes, two trees, two girls. He must see and study the objects—it is not enough to remember the objects. The definition of a Case V is "no mock-ups, only blackness." Have him continue this process until he is alert. Use liberally and often.

Then exteriorize by having the preclear close his eyes and move actual places on Earth under him, preferably places he has not been. Have him bring these up to him, find two similar things in the scene and observe the difference between them. Move him over oceans and cities until he is certain that he is exteriorized.

Then, preferably while exteriorized, have him do Step I.

This case has to *know* before he can *be*. His viewpoint is in the past. Give him present time viewpoints until he is a Step I by the methods given for Step V.

COMMENT: Present Time Differentiation is a very good general technique and resolves chronic somatics and improves tone.

Assume other people's viewpoints as a drill—not what they think about things, but as they look at things in the material universe. Attempt to be in the location of a leaf, blade of grass, car headlamp, etc., and view the universe.

Step VI: ARC Straightwire

ARC Straightwire using next-to-last list of *Self Analysis in Scientology* (which asks the preclear to recall something really real to him, etc.). Then use the lists in *Self Analysis.* This level is the neurotic. It is identified by the preclear having mock-ups which will not persist or which won't go away. Use also Present Time Differentiation. Then go to Step IV. At any drop in tone, return case to Step VI.

Step VII: Psychotic Cases

(Whether in or out of body.) The psychotic appears to be in such desperate straits that the auditor often errs in thinking desperate measures are necessary. Use the lightest possible methods. Give case space and freedom where possible. Have psychotic *imitate* (not mock-up) various things. Have him do Present Time Differentiation. Get him to tell the difference between things by actual touch. Have him locate, differentiate and touch things that are really real to him (real objects or items). If inaccessible, mimic him with own body, whatever he does, until he comes into communication. Have him locate corners of the room and hold them without thinking. As soon as his communication is up, go to Step VI. But be very sure he changes any mock-up around until he knows it is a mock-up, that it exists and that he himself made it. Do not run engrams. He is psychotic because viewpoints in present time are so scarce that he has gone into the past for viewpoints which at least he knew existed. By Present Time Differentiation, by tactile on objects, restore his idea of an abundance of viewpoint in present time. If he has been given electric shock, do not process it or any other brutality. Work him for very brief periods, for his attention span is short.

Always work psychotics with another auditor or a companion present.

NOTE: All steps for all cases. If in doubt as to condition of case, test with Step VI.

NOTE: An Operating Thetan must also be able to manufacture particles of admiration and force in abundance.

Appendix to SOP 8 No. 1

(Any alterations in SOP 8 will appear in appendices as they are expected to be minor and to make no radical change in the design of the steps in general.)

Step I

The Operating Thetan must be able to manufacture and experience, to his complete satisfaction, all sensations including pain in mock-up form and all energies such as admiration and force. It will be found that some Step I cases will not be able to manufacture admiration particles.

Step II

Be very careful not to make a lower-step preclear, while still in a body, mock-up his own body too long. Any mock-up will appear if it is simply put there often enough and long enough—providing the preclear doesn't spin in the process. The long-term manufacture of mock-ups of one's own body and of admiration may not produce quite the results expected—communication lines which should remain shut may open with bad results. These lines that are shut appear like hard, black cords to the preclear.

There are two types of techniques in general: *positive gain* and *negative gain* (as defined in the above text). Positive can be administered in unlimited amounts without harm. Negative gain techniques, such as the reduction of engrams and locks, Double Terminaling, Black and White, are often limited in the length of time they can be given. After a few hundred hours of early-type auditing, the case could be found to slump.

Thus we have in positive gain the *unlimited* technique which improves the analytical mind. In negative gain we have a *limited* (in terms of the time it can be audited) technique. In SOP 8 the following steps and processes may be audited without limit: Step I, Step III, Step V, Step VI, Step VII. The following steps are limited and should not be audited many hours without changing to another type (unlimited) for a while, after which the following steps could be resumed: Step II, Step IV. The following steps can be used on groups: Step III, Step V Part 1 and Part 2, Step VI, Step VII.

Effective Procedures

The following is a list of effective procedures as of April 28, 1953. If a procedure is labeled (U) it is unlimited and could be audited thousands of hours and only improve a case. If labeled (L) it is limited and must be handled with discretion and alternated with an unlimited technique. If it is labeled (S) it is seldom used. If labeled (A) it is used today in assists.

Engram Running, Book One (L) (A)
*Grief and other secondaries (L) (A)
Lock Scanning (L) (A)
Emotional Curves (L) (S)
Service Facsimile Chain as Engrams (L) (S)
Effort Processing (L) (A)
ARC Straightwire, *Science of Survival* (U) (A)
Negative Exteriorization (L)
Ridge Running (L)
*DED–DEDEX (L) (S) (current lifetime used for fast releases)
Motivator–Overt (L) (S)
Matched Terminals in Mock-ups (L) (S)
Double Terminals in Mock-ups (L) (A)
*Positive Exteriorization (Step I SOP 8) (U)
*Own Body Mock-up (Step II SOP 8) (L)
*Spacation (Step III SOP 8 and general usage) (U)
*Expanded GITA (Step IV SOP 8) (L)
*Present Time Differentiation (Step V SOP 8) (U)
*Exteriorization by Scenery (Step V2 SOP 8) (U)
**Self Analysis in Scientology* (Step VI SOP 8) (U)
*Imitation of Things (Step VII SOP 8) (U)
*Creative Processing (as in this book, *Scientology 8-8008*) (U)

The symbol (*) before a process above means it is recommended.

ADDITIONAL NOTE ON EXPANDED GITA: The governing rule here is that the preclear craves exactly what he has and must waste whatever he doesn't have. It is better—in the opinion of a thetan—to have anything, no matter how "bad," rather than have nothing. He craves those things which are scarce, but he can't even have those things which are scarcest. In order to have what he cannot have, he first must be able to waste it (in mock-up) in quantity. An abbreviated form of this process would involve, over and over, wasting, accepting under duress, the following items in turn:

Try first: *Healthy Bodies, Strong Bodies, Good Perception, Good Recall, Viewpoints, Pain, Work, Freedom for Others to Have Viewpoints.*

The preclear cannot be free himself until he has freed others. This does not work out in the MEST universe, but it works out in mock-ups.

Circuits go into action on many of these processes: Don't permit your preclear to think, don't be interested in what he thinks—failure to follow this rule will cause the process to fail.

Comparison of MEST objects to mock-ups resolves why thetans make facsimiles and discloses to the preclear the mechanism. This is a good process and can be done at Step IV as an additional part of IV. Have preclear make a mock-up the same as a MEST object and put the mock-up alongside of the MEST object and then compare them. The mock-ups will gradually improve, then key-out the mechanism that makes facsimiles.

Appendix to SOP 8 No. 2

Certainty Processing

The anatomy of "maybe" consists of uncertainties and is resolved by the processing of certainties. It is not resolved by the processing of uncertainties.

This Is Scientology is recommended to you for your processing and your public representation. It contains the anatomy of certainty.

An uncertainty is held in suspense solely because the preclear is holding on so hard to certainties. The basic thing he is holding on to is, "I have a solution," "I have no solution." One of these is positive, the other is negative. A complete positive and a complete negative are, alike, a certainty. The basic certainty is, "There is something," "There is nothing." A person can be certain there is something, he can be certain there is nothing.

"There is something," "There is nothing" resolves chronic somatics in this order.

One gets the preclear to have the center of the somatics say:

"There is something here,"
"There is nothing here."

Then he gets the center of the somatic to say:

"There is nothing there,"
"There is something there."

Then the auditor has the preclear say toward the somatic:

"There is something there,"
"There is nothing there."

And then he gets the preclear to say, about himself:

"There is something here,"
"There is nothing here."

This is a very fast resolution of chronic somatics. Quite ordinarily three or four minutes of this will resolve an acute state and fifteen or twenty minutes of it will resolve a chronic state.

This matter of certainties goes further. It has been determined by my recent investigations that the reason behind what is happening is the desire of a *cause* to bring about an *effect*. Something is better than nothing, anything is better than nothing. Any circuit, any effect, any anything is better than nothing. If you will Match Terminals in brackets "There is nothing," you will find that a lot of your preclears become very ill. This should be turned around into "There is something."

The way one does Matched Terminals is to have the preclear facing the preclear or his father facing his father — in other words, two of each of anything, one facing the other. These two things will discharge, one into the other, thus running off the difficulty. By "bracket" we mean, of course, running this with:

The preclear putting them up as *himself to himself;*

As though they were put up by *somebody else* (the *somebody else facing the somebody else*);

And the matched terminal again put up by *others facing others.*

The clue to all this is positive and negative, in terms of certainties. The positive plus the negative in conflict make an uncertainty. A great number of combinations of things can be run. Here's a list of the combinations.

The button behind sex is:

"I can begin life anew,"
"I cannot begin life anew."

"I can make life persist,"
"I cannot make life persist."

"I can stop life,"
"I cannot stop life."

"I can change life,"
"I cannot change life."

"I can start life,"
"I cannot start life."

A very effective process is:

"Something wrong _____ ,"
"Nothing wrong _____ ," with *you, me, them, my mind, communication,* various allies.

A very basic resolution of the lack of space of an individual is to locate these people and these objects which you've been using as anchor points (such as father, mother and so forth) and putting them into Matched Terminal brackets with this:

"There is father,"
"There is no father."

"There is grandfather,"
"There is no grandfather."

In the compulsive line this can be changed to:

"There must be no father,"
"There must be a father."

One takes all the allies of an individual and runs them in this fashion.

The basic law underneath this is that a person becomes the effect of anything upon which he has had to depend.

This would tell you immediately that the Sixth Dynamic, the MEST universe, is the largest dependency of the individual. This can be run out, but then any dynamic can be run out in this fashion:

"There is myself,"
"There is no self."

And so on, up the dynamics.

"(Any dynamic) is preventing me from communicating,"
"(Any dynamic) is not preventing me from communicating,"
is intensely effective.

Any such technique can be varied by applying the Sub-zero Scale.

One runs any certainty out because he knows that for this certainty there is an opposite negative certainty and that between these lies a "maybe" and that the maybe stays in suspense in time. The basic operation of the reactive mind is to solve problems. It is based on uncertainties about observation. Thus one runs out certainties of observation. The most general shotgun technique would have to do with:

"There is sex,"
"There is no sex."

"There is force,"
"There is no force."

This could be run, of course, in terms of Matched Terminal brackets or even as concepts. But one must not neglect to run the overt act phenomenon (which is to say, getting somebody else getting the concept).

The processing out of certainties would then embrace:

"I have a solution,"
"There is no solution."

These two opposite ends would take care of any individual who was hung on the track with some solution, for that solution had its opposite. People who have studied medicine begin by being certain that medicine works and end by being certain that medicine doesn't work. They begin by studying psychology on a supposition that it is the solution and finish up believing that it is not the solution. This also happens to superficial students of Dianetics and Scientology. Thus, one should also run:

"Dianetics is a solution,"
"Dianetics is not the solution."

This would get one off the maybe on the subject.

We are essentially processing communications systems. The entire process of auditing is concentrated upon withdrawing communications from the preclear, as predicated on the basis of the body and the preclear cannot handle communications.

Thus:

"The preclear can handle communications,"
"The preclear cannot handle communications," is a shotgun technique which resolves maybes about his communications.

An intensely interesting aspect of Certainty Processing is that it shows up intimately where the preclear is aberrated. Here is the overall basic technique. One runs:

"There is _____,"
"There is not _____," the following: *communication, talk, letters, love, agreement, sex, pain, work, bodies, minds, curiosity,*

control, enforcement, compulsion, inhibition, food, money, people, ability, beauty, ugliness, presents, and both the top and bottom of the Chart of Attitudes, positive and negative in each one.

Basic in all this is the urge of the preclear to produce an effect, so one can run:

"I can produce an effect upon Mama,"

"I cannot produce an effect upon Mama," and so forth for all allies and one will resolve the fixations of attention on the part of the preclear.

Thus fixations of attention are resolved by Certainty Processing, processing out the production of effect.

One can occasionally, if he so desires, process the direct center of the maybe (which is to say, doubt itself) in terms of Matched Terminals. This, however, is risky—for it throws the preclear into a general state of doubt.

The key to any such processing is the recovery of viewpoints.

"I can have grandfather's viewpoint,"

"I cannot have grandfather's viewpoint," and so on, particularly with sexual partners, will prove intensely interesting on a case.

"There are viewpoints,"
"There are no viewpoints."

"I have a viewpoint,"
"I don't have a viewpoint."

"_____ has a viewpoint,"
"_____ has no viewpoint," resolves problems.

One should also realize that when one is processing facsimiles, he is processing at one time energy, sensation and aesthetics.

The facsimile is a picture. The preclear is being affected by pictures, mainly, and so:

"There are no pictures,"

"There are pictures," forward the case toward handling pictures (which is to say, facsimiles).

A person tends to ally himself with somebody whom he considers capable of producing greater effects than himself, so:

"(I, she, he, it) can create greater effects,"

"(I, she, he, it) can create no effect," should be run.

When one is processing, he is trying to withdraw communications. Reach and Withdraw are the two fundamentals in the action of theta. Must Reach and Can't Reach, Must Withdraw and Can't Withdraw are compulsions which, when run in combination, produce the manifestation of insanity in a preclear.

"I can reach,"

"I can't reach."

"I can withdraw,"

"I can't withdraw," open up into the fact that remembering and forgetting are dependent upon the ability to reach and withdraw.

You will find that a preclear will respond to:

"You must _____"

or

"You can _____,"

"You must not _____"

or

"You cannot _____."

"There is _____,"
"There is not _____," forgetting and remembering.

The only reason a person is hanging on to a body or facsimile is that he has lost his belief in his ability to create. The rehabilitation of this ability to create is resolved, for instance, in a person who has had an ambition to write, with:

"I can write,"
"I cannot write," and so forth.

The loss of this creative ability made the person hang on to what he had. The fact that a preclear has forgotten how to or no longer can himself generate force, makes him hold on to stores of force. These are very often mistaken by the auditor for facsimiles. The preclear doesn't care for the facsimile. He simply cares for the force contained in the facsimile because he knows he doesn't have any force anymore.

It should be kept in mind that Reaching and Withdrawing are intensely productive of reaction in a preclear. But that preclear who does not respond to Reaching and Withdrawing and Certainty thereon, is hung up in a very special condition: *he is trying to prevent something from happening.* He also prevents auditing from happening. He has lost allies, he has had accidents and he's hung up at all those points on the track where he feels he should have prevented something from happening. This is resolved by running:

"I must prevent it from happening,"
"I cannot prevent it from happening."

"I must regain control,"
"I must lose all control."

Blackness is the desire to be an effect and the inability to be cause.

"I can create grandfather (or ally),"
"I cannot create grandfather (or ally)," solves scarcity of allies.

"I want to be aware,"
"I want no awareness," is a technique which is basic in attitudes.

Run this as others, in Matched Terminal brackets or in Expanded GITA:

"Certainty there is a past,"
"Certainty there is no past."

"Certainty there is a future,"
"Certainty there is no future."

"Certainty it means something else,"
"Certainty it does not mean anything else."

"Certainty there is space,"
"Certainty there is no space."

"Certainty there is energy,"
"Certainty there is no energy."

"Certainty there are objects,"
"Certainty there are no objects."

∞

Appendix

FURTHER STUDY
BOOKS & LECTURES BY L. RON HUBBARD

The materials of Dianetics and Scientology comprise the largest body of information ever assembled on the mind, spirit and life, rigorously refined and codified by L. Ron Hubbard through five decades of research, investigation and development. The results of that work are contained in hundreds of books and more than 3,000 recorded lectures. A full listing and description of them all can be obtained from any Scientology Church or Publications Organization. (See *Guide to the Materials*.)

The books and lectures below form the foundation upon which the Bridge to Freedom is built. They are listed in the sequence Ron wrote or delivered them. In many instances, Ron gave a series of lectures immediately following the release of a new book to provide further explanation and insight of these milestones. Through monumental restoration efforts, those lectures are now available and are listed herein with their companion book.

While Ron's books contain the summaries of breakthroughs and conclusions as they appeared in the developmental research track, his lectures provide the running day-to-day record of research and explain the thoughts, conclusions, tests and demonstrations that lay along that route. In that regard, they are the complete record of the entire research track, providing not only the most important breakthroughs in Man's history, but the *why* and *how* Ron arrived at them.

Not the least advantage of a chronological study of these books and lectures is the inclusion of words and terms which, when originally used, were defined by LRH with considerable exactitude. Far beyond a mere "definition," entire lectures are devoted to a full description of each new Dianetic or Scientology term—what made the breakthrough possible, its application in auditing as well as its application to life itself. As a result, one leaves behind no misunderstoods, obtains a full conceptual understanding of Dianetics and Scientology and grasps the subjects at a level not otherwise possible.

Through a sequential study, you can see how the subject progressed and recognize the highest levels of development. The listing of books and lectures below shows where *Scientology 8-8008* fits within the developmental line. From there you can determine your *next* step or any earlier books and lectures you may have missed. You will then be able to fill in missing gaps, not only gaining knowledge of each breakthrough, but greater understanding of what you've already studied.

This is the path to knowing how to know, unlocking the gates to your future eternity. Follow it.

DIANETICS: THE ORIGINAL THESIS • Ron's *first* description of Dianetics. Originally circulated in manuscript form, it was soon copied and passed from hand to hand. Ensuing word of mouth created such demand for more information, Ron concluded the only way to answer the inquiries was with a book. That book was Dianetics: The Modern Science of Mental Health, now the all-time self-help bestseller. Find out what started it all. For here is the bedrock foundation of Dianetic discoveries: the *Original Axioms*, the *Dynamic Principle of Existence*, the *Anatomy of the Analytical* and *Reactive Mind*, the *Dynamics*, the *Tone Scale*, the *Auditor's Code* and the first description of a *Clear*. Even more than that, here are the primary laws describing *how* and *why* auditing works. It's only here in Dianetics: The Original Thesis.

DIANETICS: THE EVOLUTION OF A SCIENCE • This is the story of *how* Ron discovered the reactive mind and developed the procedures to get rid of it. Originally written for a national magazine—published to coincide with the release of Dianetics: The Modern Science of Mental Health— it started a wildfire movement virtually overnight upon that book's publication. Here then are both the fundamentals of Dianetics as well as the only account of Ron's two-decade journey of discovery and how he applied a scientific methodology to the problems of the human mind. He wrote it so you would know. Hence, this book is a must for every Dianeticist and Scientologist.

DIANETICS: THE MODERN SCIENCE OF MENTAL HEALTH • The bolt from the blue that began a worldwide movement. For while Ron had previously announced his discovery of the reactive mind, it had only fueled the fire of those wanting more information. More to the point—it was humanly impossible for one man to clear an entire planet. Encompassing all his previous discoveries and case histories of those breakthroughs in application, Ron provided the complete handbook of Dianetics procedure to train auditors to use it everywhere. A bestseller for more than half a century and with tens of millions of copies in print, Dianetics: The Modern Science of Mental Health has been translated in more than fifty languages, and used in more than 100 countries of Earth—indisputably, the most widely read and influential book about the human mind ever written. And that is why it will forever be known as *Book One*.

> **DIANETICS LECTURES AND DEMONSTRATIONS** • Immediately following the publication of *Dianetics,* LRH began lecturing to packed auditoriums across America. Although addressing thousands at a time, demand continued to grow. To meet that demand, his presentation in Oakland, California, was recorded. In these four lectures, Ron related the events that sparked his investigation and his personal journey to his groundbreaking discoveries. He followed it all with a personal demonstration of Dianetics auditing—the only such demonstration of Book One available. *4 lectures.*

FURTHER
STUDY

DIANETICS PROFESSIONAL COURSE LECTURES — *A SPECIAL COURSE FOR BOOK ONE AUDITORS* • Following six months of coast-to-coast travel, lecturing to the first Dianeticists, Ron assembled auditors in Los Angeles for a new Professional Course. The subject was his next sweeping discovery on life — the *ARC Triangle,* describing the interrelationship of *Affinity, Reality* and *Communication.* Through a series of fifteen lectures, LRH announced many firsts, including the *Spectrum of Logic,* containing an infinity of gradients from right to wrong; *ARC and the Dynamics;* the *Tone Scales of ARC;* the *Auditor's Code* and how it relates to ARC; and the *Accessibility Chart* that classifies a case and how to process it. Here, then, is both the final statement on Book One Auditing Procedures and the discovery upon which all further research would advance. The data in these lectures was thought to be lost for over fifty years and only available in student notes published in Notes on the Lectures. The original recordings have now been discovered making them broadly available for the first time. Life in its highest state, *Understanding,* is composed of Affinity, Reality and Communication. And, as LRH said, the best description of the ARC Triangle to be found anywhere is in these lectures. *15 lectures.*

SCIENCE OF SURVIVAL — *PREDICTION OF HUMAN BEHAVIOR* • The most useful book you will ever own. Built around the *Hubbard Chart of Human Evaluation,* Science of Survival provides the first accurate prediction of human behavior. Included on the chart are all the manifestations of an individual's survival potential graduated from highest to lowest, making this the complete book on the Tone Scale. Knowing only one or two characteristics of a person and using this chart, you can plot his or her position on the Tone Scale and thereby know the rest, obtaining an accurate index of their *entire* personality, conduct and character. Before this book the world was convinced that cases could not improve but only deteriorate. Science of Survival presents the idea of different states of case and the brand-new idea that one can progress upward on the Tone Scale. And therein lies the basis of today's Grade Chart.

THE SCIENCE OF SURVIVAL LECTURES • Underlying the development of the Tone Scale and Chart of Human Evaluation was a monumental breakthrough: The *Theta–MEST Theory,* containing the explanation of the interaction between Life — *theta* — with the physical universe of Matter, Energy, Space and Time — *MEST.* In these lectures, delivered to students immediately following publication of the book, Ron gave the most expansive description of all that lies behind the Chart of Human Evaluation and its application in life itself. Moreover, here also is the explanation of how the ratio of *theta* and *en(turbulated)-theta* determines one's position on the Tone Scale and the means to ascend to higher states. *4 lectures.*

SELF ANALYSIS • The barriers of life are really just shadows. Learn to know yourself—not just a shadow of yourself. Containing the most complete description of consciousness, Self Analysis takes you through your past, through your potentials, your life. First, with a series of self-examinations and using a special version of the Hubbard Chart of Human Evaluation, you plot yourself on the Tone Scale. Then, applying a series of light yet powerful processes, you embark on the great adventure of self-discovery. This book further contains embracive principles that reach *any* case, from the lowest to the highest—including auditing techniques so effective they are referred to by Ron again and again through all following years of research into the highest states. In sum, this book not only moves one up the Tone Scale but can pull a person out of almost anything.

ADVANCED PROCEDURE AND AXIOMS • With new breakthroughs on the nature and anatomy of engrams—"Engrams are effective only when the individual himself determines that they will be effective"—came the discovery of the being's use of a *Service Facsimile:* a mechanism employed to explain away failures in life, but which then locks a person into detrimental patterns of behavior and further failure. In consequence came a new type of processing addressing *Thought, Emotion* and *Effort* detailed in the "Fifteen Acts" of Advanced Procedure and oriented to the rehabilitation of the preclear's *Self-determinism.* Hence, this book also contains the all-encompassing, no-excuses-allowed explanation of *Full Responsibility,* the key to unlocking it all. Moreover, here is the codification of *Definitions, Logics,* and *Axioms,* providing both the summation of the entire subject and direction for all future research. *See Handbook for Preclears, written as a companion self-processing manual to Advanced Procedure and Axioms.*

> **THOUGHT, EMOTION AND EFFORT** • With the codification of the Axioms came the means to address key points on a case that could unravel all aberration. *Basic Postulates, Prime Thought, Cause and Effect* and their effect on everything from *memory* and *responsibility* to an individual's own role in empowering *engrams*—these matters are only addressed in this series. Here, too, is the most complete description of the *Service Facsimile* found anywhere—and why its resolution removes an individual's self-imposed disabilities. *21 lectures.*

HANDBOOK FOR PRECLEARS • The "Fifteen Acts" of Advanced Procedure and Axioms are paralleled by the fifteen Self-processing Acts given in Handbook for Preclears. Moreover, this book contains several essays giving the most expansive description of the *Ideal State of Man*. Discover why behavior patterns become so solidly fixed; why habits seemingly can't be broken; how decisions long ago have more power over a person than his decisions today; and why a person keeps past negative experiences in the present. It's all clearly laid out on the Chart of Attitudes—a milestone breakthrough that complements the Chart of Human Evaluation—plotting the ideal state of being and one's *attitudes* and *reactions* to life. *In self-processing, Handbook for Preclears is used in conjunction with Self Analysis.*

THE LIFE CONTINUUM • Besieged with requests for lectures on his latest breakthroughs, Ron replied with everything they wanted and more at the Second Annual Conference of Dianetic Auditors. Describing the technology that lies behind the self-processing steps of the *Handbook*—here is the *how* and *why* of it all: the discovery of *Life Continuum*—the mechanism by which an individual is compelled to carry on the life of another deceased or departed individual, generating in his own body the infirmities and mannerisms of the departed. Combined with auditor instruction on use of the Chart of Attitudes in determining how to enter every case at the proper gradient, here, too, are directions for dissemination of the Handbook and hence, the means to begin wide-scale clearing. *10 lectures.*

SCIENTOLOGY: MILESTONE ONE • Ron began the first lecture in this series with six words that would change the world forever: "This is a course in *Scientology*." From there, Ron not only described the vast scope of this, a then brand-new subject, he also detailed his discoveries on past lives. He proceeded from there to the description of the first E-Meter and its initial use in uncovering the *theta line* (the entire track of a thetan's existence), as entirely distinct from the *genetic body line* (the time track of bodies and their physical evolution), shattering the "one-life" lie and revealing the *whole track* of spiritual existence. Here, then, is the very genesis of Scientology. *22 lectures.*

THE ROUTE TO INFINITY: TECHNIQUE 80 LECTURES • As Ron explained, "Technique 80 is the *To Be or Not To Be* Technique." With that, he unveiled the crucial foundation on which ability and sanity rest: *the being's capacity to make a decision*. Here, then, is the anatomy of "maybe," the *Wavelengths of ARC,* the *Tone Scale of Decisions,* and the means to rehabilitate a being's ability *To Be* … almost *anything. 7 lectures. (Knowledge of Technique 80 is required for Technique 88 as described in Scientology: A History of Man —below.)*

SCIENTOLOGY: A HISTORY OF MAN • "A cold-blooded and factual account of your last 76 trillion years." So begins A History of Man, announcing the revolutionary *Technique 88* —revealing for the first time the truth about whole track experience and the exclusive address, in auditing, to the thetan. Here is history unraveled with the first E-Meter, delineating and describing the principal incidents on the whole track to be found in any human being: *Electronic implants, entities,* the *genetic track, between-lives incidents, how bodies evolved* and *why you got trapped in them* —they're all detailed here.

> **TECHNIQUE 88: INCIDENTS ON THE TRACK BEFORE EARTH** •
> "Technique 88 is the most hyperbolical, effervescent, dramatic, unexaggeratable, high-flown, superlative, grandiose, colossal and magnificent technique which the mind of Man could conceivably embrace. It is as big as the whole track and all the incidents on it. It's what you apply it to; it's what's been going on. It contains the riddles and secrets, the mysteries of all time. You could bannerline this technique like they do a sideshow, but nothing you could say, no adjective you could use, would adequately describe even a small segment of it. It not only batters the imagination, it makes you ashamed to imagine anything," is Ron's introduction to you in this never-before-available lecture series, expanding on all else contained in History of Man. What awaits you is the whole track itself. *15 lectures.*

SCIENTOLOGY 8-80 • The *first* explanation of the electronics of human thought and the energy phenomena in any being. Discover how even physical universe laws of motion are mirrored in a being, not to mention the electronics of aberration. Here is the link between theta and MEST revealing what energy *is,* and how you *create* it. It was this breakthrough that revealed the subject of a thetan's *flows* and which, in turn, is applied in *every* auditing process today. In the book's title, "8-8" stands for *Infinity-Infinity,* and "0" represents the static, *theta.* Included are the *Wavelengths of Emotion, Aesthetics, Beauty and Ugliness, Inflow and Outflow* and the *Sub-zero Tone Scale* —applicable only to the thetan.

> **SOURCE OF LIFE ENERGY** • Beginning with the announcement of his
> new book — Scientology 8-80 —Ron not only unveiled his breakthroughs of theta as the Source of Life Energy, but detailed the *Methods of Research* he used to make that and every other discovery of Dianetics and Scientology: the *Qs* and *Logics* —methods of *thinking* applicable to any universe or thinking process. Here, then, is both *how to think* and *how to evaluate all data and knowledge,* and thus, the linchpin to a full understanding of both Scientology and life itself. *14 lectures.*

FURTHER
STUDY

🎙 THE COMMAND OF THETA • While in preparation of his newest book and the Doctorate Course he was about to deliver, Ron called together auditors for a new Professional Course. As he said, "For the first time with this class we are stepping, really, beyond the scope of the word *Survival*." From that vantage point, the Command of Theta gives the technology that bridges the knowledge from 8-80 to 8-8008, and provides the first full explanation of the subject of *Cause* and a permanent shift of orientation in life from MEST to *Theta*. *10 lectures.*

SCIENTOLOGY 8-8008 • *(This current volume.)* The complete description of the behavior and potentials of a *thetan,* and textbook for the Philadelphia Doctorate Course and The Factors: Admiration and the Renaissance of Beingness lectures. As Ron said, the book's title serves to fix in the mind of the individual a route by which he can rehabilitate himself, his abilities, his ethics and his goals—the attainment of *infinity* (8) by the reduction of the apparent *infinity* (8) of the MEST universe to *zero* (0) and the increase of the apparent *zero* (0) of one's own universe to *infinity* (8). Condensed herein are more than 80,000 hours of investigation, with a summarization and amplification of every breakthrough to date—and the full significance of those discoveries form the new vantage point of *Operating Thetan.*

🎙 THE PHILADELPHIA DOCTORATE COURSE LECTURES • This renowned series stands as the largest single body of work on the anatomy, behavior and potentials of the spirit of Man ever assembled, providing the very fundamentals which underlie the route to Operating Thetan. Here it is in complete detail—the thetan's relationship to the *creation, maintenance* and *destruction of universes.* In just those terms, here is the *anatomy* of matter, energy, space and time, and *postulating* universes into existence. Here, too, is the thetan's fall from whole track abilities and the *universal laws* by which they are restored. In short, here is Ron's codification of the upper echelon of theta beingness and behavior. Lecture after lecture fully expands every concept of the course text, Scientology 8-8008, providing the total scope of *you* in native state. *76 lectures and accompanying reproductions of the original 54 LRH hand-drawn lecture charts.*

🎙 THE FACTORS: ADMIRATION AND THE RENAISSANCE OF BEINGNESS • With the *potentials* of a thetan fully established came a look outward resulting in Ron's monumental discovery of a *universal solvent* and the basic laws of the theta *universe*—laws quite literally senior to anything: *The Factors: Summation of the Considerations of the Human Spirit and Material Universe.* So dramatic were these breakthroughs, Ron expanded the book Scientology 8-8008, both clarifying previous discoveries and adding chapter after chapter which, studied with these lectures, provide a postgraduate level to the Doctorate Course. Here then are lectures containing the knowledge of *universal truth* unlocking the riddle of creation itself. *18 lectures.*

SCIENTOLOGY 8-8008
L. RON HUBBARD

THE CREATION OF HUMAN ABILITY — *A HANDBOOK FOR SCIENTOLOGISTS* • On the heels of his discoveries of Operating Thetan came a year of intensive research, exploring the realm of a *thetan exterior.* Through auditing and instruction, including 450 lectures in this same twelve-month span, Ron codified the entire subject of Scientology. And it's all contained in this handbook, from a *Summary of Scientology* to its basic *Axioms* and *Codes.* Moreover, here is *Intensive Procedure,* containing the famed Exteriorization Processes of *Route 1* and *Route 2* — processes drawn right from the Axioms. Each one is described in detail — *how* the process is used, *why* it works, the axiomatic technology that underlies its use, and the complete explanation of how a being can break the *false agreements* and *self-created barriers* that enslave him to the physical universe. In short, this book contains the ultimate summary of thetan exterior OT ability and its permanent accomplishment.

PHOENIX LECTURES: FREEING THE HUMAN SPIRIT • Here is the panoramic view of Scientology complete. Having codified the subject of Scientology in Creation of Human Ability, Ron then delivered a series of half-hour lectures to specifically accompany a full study of the book. From the *essentials* that underlie the technology — *The Axioms, Conditions of Existence* and *Considerations and Mechanics,* to the processes of *Intensive Procedure,* including twelve lectures describing one-by-one the thetan exterior processes of *Route 1* — it's all covered in full, providing a conceptual understanding of the *science of knowledge* and *native state OT ability.* Here then are the bedrock principles upon which everything in Scientology rests, including the embracive statement of the religion and its heritage — *Scientology, Its General Background.* Hence, this is the watershed lecture series on Scientology itself, and the axiomatic foundation for all future research. *42 lectures.*

DIANETICS 55! — *THE COMPLETE MANUAL OF HUMAN COMMUNICATION* • With all breakthroughs to date, a single factor had been isolated as crucial to success in every type of auditing. As LRH said, "Communication is so thoroughly important today in Dianetics and Scientology (as it always has been on the whole track) that it could be said if you were to get a preclear into communication, you would get him well." And this book delineates the *exact,* but previously unknown, anatomy and formulas for *perfect* communication. The magic of the communication cycle is *the* fundamental of auditing and the primary reason auditing works. The breakthroughs here opened new vistas of application — discoveries of such magnitude, LRH called Dianetics 55! the *Second Book* of Dianetics.

THE UNIFICATION CONGRESS: COMMUNICATION! FREEDOM & ABILITY • The historic Congress announcing the reunification of the subjects of Dianetics and Scientology with the release of *Dianetics 55!* Until now, each had operated in their own sphere: Dianetics addressed Man *as Man* — the first four dynamics, while Scientology addressed *life itself* — the Fifth to Eighth Dynamics. The formula which would serve as the foundation for all future development was contained in a single word: *Communication.* It was a paramount breakthrough Ron would later call, "the great discovery of Dianetics and Scientology." Here, then, are the lectures, as it happened. *16 lectures and accompanying reproductions of the original LRH hand-drawn lecture charts.*

322

SCIENTOLOGY: THE FUNDAMENTALS OF THOUGHT—*THE BASIC BOOK OF THE THEORY AND PRACTICE OF SCIENTOLOGY FOR BEGINNERS* • Designated by Ron as the *Book One of Scientology.* After having fully unified and codified the subjects of Dianetics and Scientology came the refinement of their *fundamentals.* Originally published as a résumé of Scientology for use in translations into non-English tongues, this book is of inestimable value to both the beginner and advanced student of the mind, spirit and life. Equipped with this book alone, one can begin a practice and perform seeming miracle changes in the states of well-being, ability and intelligence of people. Contained within are the *Conditions of Existence, Eight Dynamics, ARC Triangle, Parts of Man,* the full analysis of *Life as a Game,* and more, including exact processes for individual application of these principles in processing. Here, then, in one book, is the starting point for bringing Scientology to people everywhere.

HUBBARD PROFESSIONAL COURSE LECTURES • While Fundamentals of Thought stands as an introduction to the subject for beginners, it also contains a distillation of fundamentals for every Scientologist. Here are the in-depth descriptions of those fundamentals, each lecture one-half hour in length and providing, one-by-one, a complete mastery of a single Scientology breakthrough—*Axioms 1–10; The Anatomy of Control; Handling of Problems; Start, Change and Stop; Confusion and Stable Data; Exteriorization; Valences* and more—the *why* behind them, *how* they came to be and their mechanics. And it's all brought together with the *Code of a Scientologist,* point by point, and its use in actually creating a new civilization. In short, here are the LRH lectures that make a *Professional Scientologist*—one who can apply the subject to every aspect of life. *21 lectures.*

ADDITIONAL BOOKS CONTAINING SCIENTOLOGY ESSENTIALS

WORK

THE PROBLEMS OF WORK—*SCIENTOLOGY APPLIED TO THE WORKADAY WORLD* • Having codified the entire subject of Scientology, Ron immediately set out to provide the *beginning* manual for its application by anyone. As he described it: life is composed of seven-tenths work, one-tenth familial, one-tenth political and one-tenth relaxation. Here, then, is Scientology applied to that seven-tenths of existence including the answers to *Exhaustion* and the *Secret of Efficiency.* Here, too, is the analysis of life itself—a game composed of exact rules. Know them and you succeed. Problems of Work contains technology no one can live without, and that can immediately be applied by both the Scientologist and those new to the subject.

LIFE PRINCIPLES

SCIENTOLOGY: A NEW SLANT ON LIFE • Scientology essentials for every aspect of life. Basic answers that put you in charge of your existence, truths to consult again and again: *Is It Possible to Be Happy?, Two Rules for Happy Living, Personal Integrity, The Anti-Social Personality* and many more. In every part of this book you will find Scientology truths that describe conditions in your life and furnish *exact* ways to improve them. Scientology: A New Slant on Life contains essential knowledge for every Scientologist and a perfect introduction for anyone new to the subject.

AXIOMS, CODES AND SCALES

SCIENTOLOGY 0-8: THE BOOK OF BASICS • The companion to *all* Ron's books, lectures and materials. This is *the* Book of Basics, containing indispensable data you will refer to constantly: the *Axioms of Dianetics and Scientology; The Factors;* a full compilation of all *Scales*—more than 100 in all; listings of the *Perceptics* and *Awareness Levels;* all *Codes* and *Creeds* and much more. The senior laws of existence are condensed into this single volume, distilled from more than 15,000 pages of writings, 3,000 lectures and scores of books.

$\mathscr{S}$CIENTOLOGY ETHICS:
TECHNOLOGY OF OPTIMUM SURVIVAL

INTRODUCTION TO SCIENTOLOGY ETHICS • A new hope for Man arises with the first workable technology of ethics—technology to help an individual pull himself out of the downward skid of life and to a higher plateau of survival. This is the comprehensive handbook providing the crucial fundamentals: *Basics of Ethics & Justice; Honesty; Conditions of Existence; Condition Formulas* from Confusion to Power; the *Basics of Suppression* and its handling; as well as *Justice Procedures* and their use in Scientology Churches. Here, then, is the technology to overcome any barriers in life and in one's personal journey up the Bridge to Total Freedom.

$\mathscr{P}$URIFICATION

CLEAR BODY, CLEAR MIND—*THE EFFECTIVE PURIFICATION PROGRAM* • We live in a biochemical world, and this book is the solution. While investigating the harmful effects that earlier drug use had on preclears' cases, Ron made the major discovery that many street drugs, particularly LSD, remained in a person's body long after ingested. Residues of the drug, he noted, could have serious and lasting effects, including triggering further "trips." Additional research revealed that a wide range of substances—medical drugs, alcohol, pollutants, household chemicals and even food preservatives—could also lodge in the body's tissues. Through research on thousands of cases, he developed the *Purification Program* to eliminate their destructive effects. Clear Body, Clear Mind details every aspect of the all-natural regimen that can free one from the harmful effects of drugs and other toxins, opening the way for spiritual progress.

REFERENCE HANDBOOKS

WHAT IS SCIENTOLOGY?

The complete and essential encyclopedic reference on the subject and practice of Scientology. Organized for use, this book contains the pertinent data on every aspect of the subject:

• The life of L. Ron Hubbard and his path of discovery

• The Spiritual Heritage of the religion

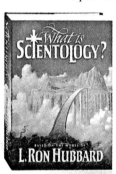

• A full description of Dianetics and Scientology

• Auditing—what it is and how it works

• Courses—what they contain and how they are structured

• The Grade Chart of Services and how one ascends to higher states

• The Scientology Ethics and Justice System

• The Organizational Structure of the Church

• A complete description of the many Social Betterment programs supported by the Church, including: Drug Rehabilitation, Criminal Reform, Literacy and Education and the instilling of real values for morality

Over 1,000 pages in length, with more than 500 photographs and illustrations, this text further includes Creeds, Codes, a full listing of all books and materials as well as a Catechism with answers to virtually any question regarding the subject.

You Ask and This Book Answers.

THE SCIENTOLOGY HANDBOOK

Scientology fundamentals for daily use in every part of life. Encompassing 19 separate bodies of technology, here is the most comprehensive manual on the basics of life ever published. Each chapter contains key principles and technology for your continual use:

• Study Technology

• The Dynamics of Existence

• The Components of Understanding—Affinity, Reality and Communication

• The Tone Scale

• Communication and its Formulas

• Assists for Illnesses and Injuries

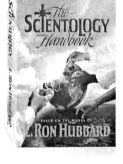

• How to Resolve Conflicts

• Integrity and Honesty

• Ethics and Condition Formulas

• Answers to Suppression and a Dangerous Environment

• Marriage

• Children

• Tools for the Workplace

More than 700 photographs and illustrations make it easy for you to learn the procedures and apply them at once. This book is truly the indispensable handbook for every Scientologist.

The Technology to Build a Better World.

ABOUT L. RON HUBBARD

"To really know life," L. Ron Hubbard wrote, "you've got to be part of life. You must get down and look, you must get into the nooks and crannies of existence. You have to rub elbows with all kinds and types of men before you can finally establish what he is."

Through his long and extraordinary journey to the founding of Dianetics and Scientology, Ron did just that. From his adventurous youth in a rough and tumble American West to his far-flung trek across a still mysterious Asia; from his two-decade search for the very essence of life to the triumph of Dianetics and Scientology—such are the stories recounted in the L. Ron Hubbard Biographical Publications.

Presenting the photographic overview of Ron's greater journey is *L. Ron Hubbard: Images of a Lifetime*. Drawn from his own archival collection, this is Ron's life as he himself saw it.

While for the many aspects of that rich and varied life, stands the Ron Series. Each issue focuses on a specific LRH profession: *Auditor, Humanitarian, Philosopher, Artist, Poet, Music Maker, Photographer* and many more including his published articles on *Freedom* and his personal *Letters & Journals*. Here is the life of a man who lived at least twenty lives in the space of one.

FOR FURTHER INFORMATION VISIT
www.lronhubbard.org

GUIDE TO THE MATERIALS

YOU'RE ON AN ADVENTURE!
HERE'S THE MAP.

- All books
- All lectures
- All reference books

All of it laid out in chronological sequence with descriptions of what each contains.

*Y*our journey to a full understanding of Dianetics and Scientology is the greatest adventure of all. But you need a map that shows you where you are and where you are going.

That map is the Materials Guide Chart. It shows all Ron's books and lectures with a full description of their content and subject matter so you can find exactly what *you* are looking for and precisely what *you* need.

Since each book and lecture is laid out in chronological sequence, you can see *how* the subjects of Dianetics and Scientology were developed. And what that means is by simply studying this chart you are in for cognition after cognition!

New editions of all books include extensive glossaries, containing definitions for every technical term. And as a result of a monumental restoration program, the entire library of Ron's lectures are being made available on compact disc, with complete transcripts, glossaries, lecture graphs, diagrams and issues he refers to in the lectures. As a result, you get *all* the data, and can learn with ease, gaining a full *conceptual* understanding.

And what that adds up to is a new Golden Age of Knowledge every Dianeticist and Scientologist has dreamed of.

To obtain your FREE Materials Guide Chart and Catalog, or to order L. Ron Hubbard's books and lectures, contact:

WESTERN HEMISPHERE:
**Bridge
Publications, Inc.**
4751 Fountain Avenue
Los Angeles, CA 90029 USA
www.bridgepub.com
Phone: 1-800-722-1733
Fax: 1-323-953-3328

EASTERN HEMISPHERE:
**New Era Publications
International ApS**
Store Kongensgade 53
1264 Copenhagen K, Denmark
www.newerapublications.com
Phone: (45) 33 73 66 66
Fax: (45) 33 73 66 33

Books and lectures are also available direct from Churches of Scientology.
*See **Addresses**.*

$\mathcal{A}$DDRESSES

$\mathcal{S}$cientology is the fastest-growing religion in the world today. Churches and Missions exist in cities throughout the world, and new ones are continually forming.

To obtain more information or to locate the Church nearest you, visit the Scientology website:

www.scientology.org
e-mail: info@scientology.org

or

Phone: 1-800-334-LIFE
(for US and Canada)

You can also write to any one of the Continental Organizations, listed on the following page, who can direct you to one of the thousands of Churches and Missions world over.

L. Ron Hubbard's books and lectures may be obtained from any of these addresses or direct from the publishers on the previous page.

CONTINENTAL CHURCH ORGANIZATIONS:

UNITED STATES

CHURCH OF SCIENTOLOGY
CONTINENTAL LIAISON OFFICE
WESTERN UNITED STATES
1308 L. Ron Hubbard Way
Los Angeles, California 90027 USA
info@wus.scientology.org

CHURCH OF SCIENTOLOGY
CONTINENTAL LIAISON OFFICE
EASTERN UNITED STATES
349 W. 48th Street
New York, New York 10036 USA
info@eus.scientology.org

CANADA

CHURCH OF SCIENTOLOGY
CONTINENTAL LIAISON OFFICE
CANADA
696 Yonge Street, 2nd Floor
Toronto, Ontario
Canada M4Y 2A7
info@scientology.ca

LATIN AMERICA

CHURCH OF SCIENTOLOGY
CONTINENTAL LIAISON OFFICE
LATIN AMERICA
Federacion Mexicana de Dianetica
Calle Puebla #31
Colonia Roma, Mexico D.F.
C.P. 06700, Mexico
info@scientology.org.mx

UNITED KINGDOM

CHURCH OF SCIENTOLOGY
CONTINENTAL LIAISON OFFICE
UNITED KINGDOM
Saint Hill Manor
East Grinstead, West Sussex
England, RH19 4JY
info@scientology.org.uk

AFRICA

CHURCH OF SCIENTOLOGY
CONTINENTAL LIAISON OFFICE AFRICA
5 Cynthia Street
Kensington
Johannesburg 2094, South Africa
info@scientology.org.za

AUSTRALIA, NEW ZEALAND & OCEANIA
CHURCH OF SCIENTOLOGY
CONTINENTAL LIAISON OFFICE ANZO
16 Dorahy Street
Dundas, New South Wales 2117
Australia
info@scientology.org.au

Church of Scientology
Liaison Office of Taiwan
1st, No. 231, Cisian 2nd Road
Kaoshiung City
Taiwan, ROC
info@scientology.org.tw

EUROPE
CHURCH OF SCIENTOLOGY
CONTINENTAL LIAISON OFFICE EUROPE
Store Kongensgade 55
1264 Copenhagen K, Denmark
info@scientology.org.dk

Church of Scientology
Liaison Office of Commonwealth
of Independent States
Management Center of Dianetics
and Scientology Dissemination
Pervomajskaya Street, House 1A
Korpus Grazhdanskoy Oboroni
Losino-Petrovsky Town
141150 Moscow, Russia
info@scientology.ru

Church of Scientology
Liaison Office of Central Europe
1082 Leonardo da Vinci u. 8-14
Budapest, Hungary
info@scientology.hu

Church of Scientology
Liaison Office of Iberia
C/Miguel Menendez Boneta, 18
28460 – Los Molinos
Madrid, Spain
info@spain.scientology.org

Church of Scientology
Liaison Office of Italy
Via Cadorna, 61
20090 Vimodrone
Milan, Italy
info@scientology.it

$\mathcal{B}$ECOME A MEMBER
OF THE INTERNATIONAL
ASSOCIATION OF SCIENTOLOGISTS

$\mathcal{T}$he International Association of Scientologists is the membership organization of all Scientologists united in the most vital crusade on Earth.

A free Six-Month Introductory Membership is extended to anyone who has not held a membership with the Association before.

As a member, you are eligible for discounts on Scientology materials offered only to IAS Members. You also receive the Association magazine, *IMPACT,* issued six times a year, full of Scientology news from around the world.

The purpose of the IAS is:

"To unite, advance, support and protect Scientology and Scientologists in all parts of the world so as to achieve the Aims of Scientology as originated by L. Ron Hubbard."

Join the strongest force for positive change on the planet today, opening the lives of millions to the greater truth embodied in Scientology.

JOIN THE INTERNATIONAL ASSOCIATION OF SCIENTOLOGISTS.

To apply for membership,
write to the International
Association of Scientologists
c/o Saint Hill Manor, East Grinstead
West Sussex, England, RH19 4JY

www.iasmembership.org

$\mathscr{E}$DITOR'S GLOSSARY
OF WORDS, TERMS AND PHRASES

Words often have several meanings. The definitions used here only give the meaning that the word has as it is used in this book. Dianetics and Scientology terms appear in bold type. Beside each definition you will find the page on which it first appears, so you can refer back to the text if you wish.

This glossary is not meant to take the place of standard language or Dianetics and Scientology dictionaries, which should be referred to for any words, terms or phrases that do not appear below.

LRH technical terms defined for Standard Operating Procedure are listed in the definitions section of Standard Operating Procedure, Issue 3, in Book One, Part Three of this book.

— The Editors

abdicating: giving up power or responsibility. Page 252.

abstraction: the idea of something which has no independent existence; a thing which exists only in idea. Page 14.

acquiescence: the act or condition of giving agreement or consent without objection or protest. Page 121.

adhesion, cohesion and: in physics, *adhesion* is the force which holds together the molecules of unlike substances. *Cohesion* is the force which makes particles or molecules of one kind of substance stick together. For example, when a sheet of glass is lowered into water and withdrawn, water will cling to it (adhesion) but the remainder will be pulled back into the main body of water (cohesion). Page 39.

admiration: approving attention given to. Admiration is fully covered in the lecture series *The Factors.* Page 239.

adulation: excessive admiration or devotion; exaggerated praise. Page 131.

a little of (something) goes a very long distance: a variation of *a little goes a long way,* a small amount of (something) can have a great effect or a strong influence on a person or thing. Page 120.

alloyed: lowered in quality or degree; corrupted by mixture. Literally, an *alloy* is a metal formed by mixing two different types of metal together or by mixing metal with another substance, thought of as not pure. Hence, *alloyed affinity* is affinity that is not pure and therefore reduced in quality. Page 138.

along the lines of: in accordance with; in the manner of. Page 259.

alternating current: electricity that flows for only a short while in one direction and then reverses to flow a short while in the opposite direction (as opposed to direct current, as in a battery). It keeps reversing or alternating back and forth at a rapid rate. For example, most electrical outlets operate on alternating current. Page 151.

amenable: willing to be influenced by somebody or something; inclined to answer, respond or submit to (somebody or something). Page 252.

anatomy: 1. a detailed examination or analysis of something. Page 16.
2. structure or arrangement of the parts of something. Page 67.

anesthesia: loss or partial loss of feeling or sensation. Page 97.

angels have two faces: a reference to an old belief in certain religions that angels or other divine beings (such as gods) have a dual aspect and are capable of both good and evil, creativity and destruction, etc. Hence, they are commonly represented in mythology as having a black and a white face. Page 127.

antipathetic: having a feeling of *antipathy,* an instinctive opposition or hostility, to something that one considers disagreeable, offensive or the like; strong or deep-rooted dislike. Page 127.

arbitrary: 1. a factor or force which does not derive from natural laws. Page 29.
2. based on judgment or useful selection rather than on the fixed nature of something. Page 37.

art: an older form of the word *are.* Page 166.

associative logic: a type of logic which borders on identification. It is built on the basis of anything given attention to will activate the whole class of things. Example: A beer keg is a beer barrel. Bigger. Which means "my brother" because he's bigger. Page 58.

as the case may be: according to the circumstances (used when referring to two or more possible alternatives). Page 40.

astral walking: the belief by spiritualists that the astral body could be separated from and journey outside the physical body and when it did so was composed of a spirit *and* mind *and* body. This is in contrast to Scientology where the thetan (spirit, the person himself) can *fully* detach, by itself, from both mind and body (exteriorization). Page 205.

at length: after some time; eventually. Page 188.

at long length: in the final analysis; ultimately; finally. Page 33.

at once (with): in one and the same way, manner, position, condition (with) etc., as in *"ARC forms a triangle which is, at once, with all three corners at a single level."* Page 42.

attain to: succeed in reaching; reach a condition or purpose. Page 119.

at the wheel of a car: operating or driving an automobile. Page 132.

attitude: an orientation or position assumed. Page 73.

avail: effective use in the achievement of a goal; advantage; use. Page 3.

back flows: a flowing back or returning in the opposite direction, likened to a fluid that flows back toward a source; a reverse flow. Page 210.

banishment: a clearing away; a getting rid of; disappearance. Page 165.

base: 1. lacking in high values or moral principles. Page 132. 2. the bottom support of anything; that on which a thing stands or rests. Page 206.

basest: appropriate to an inferior thing or being; the most degraded or degrading; the most unworthy. Page 131.

bear: exhibit; show. Page 12.

becomingness: the state or quality of *becoming,* growing or coming to be. Page 241.

begets: calls into being, gives rise to; produces. Page 253.

bestiality: sexual relations between a person and an animal. Page 296.

betoken: indicate; give evidence of. Page 202.

biology: the science of the origin, development, physical characteristics, habits, etc., of living forms. Page 3.

black band of sound: a band of sound which is supersonic (beyond human hearing) and is so intense it can destroy living tissues. Page 91.

black beyond: the vast reaches of dark outer space between galaxies in the massive dimensions of the MEST universe. *Black* here refers to the blackness of outer space where there are no suns or stars and *beyond* means that which is at a vast distance. Page 124.

black with the bones of lost beingness: hopeless and doomed as shown by the dead and decayed bodies of those who went before and failed to discover truth. *Black* in this sense means characterized by the absence of light or enveloped in darkness, and hence, the opposite of bright and hopeful. *Bones* refers to the skeletons of dead bodies, and *lost beingness* means identities that were neither discovered nor recovered. Page 122.

blazing: burning brightly and with great force; of tremendous intensity or fervor. Page 153.

blazing and crackling: refers to the look and sound one can observe near some high-powered electrical lines. *See also* **blazing** and **crackling**. Page 153.

booby-trapped: set with a hidden trap for the unsuspecting. *Booby-trap* is a military term for a harmless-looking object concealing an explosive charge, designed to go off if the object is touched. A *booby* is a person regarded as stupid. Page 205.

borne out: proven to be true. Page 25.

bracket(s): one runs things in *brackets*. The word "bracket" is taken from the artillery, meaning to enclose within a salvo (sudden burst of bullets or other projectiles) of fire. A bracket is run as follows: First, one gets the concept as *happening to the preclear.* Then, one gets the concept of *the preclear making* *it happen (or thinking or saying it) to another.* Then one gets the concept as *being directed by another at others.* Page 107.

breadth: 1. an extent or area of something; size in general. Page 23. 2. wide range or scope; freedom from narrowness. Page 106.

brink: a crucial or critical point, especially of a situation or state beyond which success or catastrophe occurs. Literally, the very edge of a steep place such as the *brink* of a cliff. Page 123.

brook: endure or put up with; tolerate. Page 58.

brotherhood: an association or alliance, such as men with men, men with other things, etc.; a feeling of closeness with something, as in *"One declines into a 'brotherhood with the universe.'"* Page 48.

brutal: extremely ruthless, harsh or cruel; savagely violent. Page 168.

buttons: those computations or foibles or quirks of the human mind which can be made right by merely touching one factor. This term comes from the idea of pushing a button to activate something, as in an electrical or mechanical device. Page 182.

by means of: through the use of; through a particular method or system; through the help of. Page 209.

by reason of: because of, due to. Page 266.

carbon batteries: batteries that utilize carbon as one of their components to produce electricity. A carbon battery consists of two different terminals: one is positive (made of carbon) and the other negative (made of zinc), the difference causing an electrical flow. Page 150.

caring to: being concerned about or interested in; willing to make an effort to do something. Page 19.

carousel: an amusement ride which consists of a revolving, circular platform with wooden horses or other animals, benches, etc., on which people may sit or ride, usually to the accompaniment of mechanical or recorded music. Hence, something that goes round and round like a carousel without actually going anywhere. Page 217.

Case V: same as Step V (five) or "V." The definition of a Case V is "no mock-ups, only blackness." The term refers to the fifth step of Standard Operating Procedure wherein the auditor tests the preclear at each stage of the process to find a step the preclear can do and begins processing at that step. A preclear who had to be started at Step V of the process was called a "Case V." Page 297.

cast off: to loosen or let go of, likened to throwing off the lines of a vessel to free it from its being tied up. Page 209.

cause: cause is potential source of flow. Page 15.

Cause: something without space, without time, without form; a true static which has the potential of creating, conserving, altering or destroying matter, energy, space and time. And that is *Cause* and it can become a noun with a capital *C*. Page 113.

chain fission: used in this book as an analogy to the chain reaction that takes place when the center portion of an atom (the nucleus) is split (fissioned) into smaller parts, with these smaller parts ejecting outward and splitting other atoms, which in turn split others and so on. Page 151.

Cleared Theta Clear: a thetan who is completely rehabilitated and can do everything a thetan should do, such as move MEST and control others from a distance, or create his own universe. Page 175.

clear of: free from obstruction, burden or limitation; disengaged from; disentangled from. Page 207.

clinical test: *clinical* means involving or based on direct observation of something or someone. A *clinical test* is something that serves as an example or a basis for evaluation. Page 228.

close gauge: a precise system of measurement for assessing something or for estimating or determining the correctness of something. Page 83.

Code of Ethics (Honor) Processing: the Code of Honor is a complete process in itself because the code is basically sane conduct. One can run such processes as Straightwire, Lock Scanning or dichotomies on each point of the code. Code of Honor Processing is covered in the lecture of 7 November 1952, "Force As Homo Sapiens and As Thetan—Responsibility" in the *Source of Life Energy* series. Page 160.

cohesion and adhesion: in physics, *cohesion* is the force which makes particles or molecules of one kind of substance stick together. *Adhesion* is the force which holds together the molecules of unlike substances. For example, when a sheet of glass is lowered into water and withdrawn, water will cling to it (adhesion) but the remainder will be pulled back into the main body of water (cohesion). Page 39.

cohesiveness: the state, condition or quality of *cohering,* uniting or sticking together. Figuratively, a nonmaterial union. Page 39.

coincidentally: in a manner that is happening or existing at the same time. Page 246.

comatose: of, pertaining to, or of the nature of a *coma,* a state of prolonged unconsciousness. Page 42.

command value: the relative effectiveness of something in directing, dictating, influencing, ordering and the like. Page 19.

commingled: mixed or brought together, usually without a loss of individual characteristics. Page 124.

common practice, in: expected, usual and customary performance. Page 18.

composite: a structure or an entity made up of distinct parts, elements or components (sometimes so combined as to lose some of their distinctive individual characters). Page 16.

compromise: 1. to come to an agreement (with another reality) by the partial surrender of one's own position, principles or standards. Page 138.
2. the result of yielding or adjusting, such as to a lowering of quality, standard, etc. Page 260.

comrade: a person who shares in one's activities, occupation, fortunes or experiences; close friend or companion. Page 137.

Concepts and Feelings: a processing technique which has the preclear get and hold a particular concept and feeling until it blows. The concept is an idea and the feeling is an emotion, and one can get both at the same time. As an example, "Get the idea of dying" is a concept. "The beautiful sadness of dying" is holding the concept of dying and the emotion of beautiful sadness. The preclear will feel, as he holds the concept, the emotional level change, and the thing will blow. Concepts and Feelings is described in *Scientology 8-80.* Page 160.

concert: to contrive or arrange by agreement. Page 120.

concourse: communication; interchange. From *con* meaning together, and *course* meaning to flow. Page 241.

condenser: a device for accumulating and holding electrical charge. A condenser consists of two equally but oppositely charged conducting surfaces held apart by insulating material. Page 150.

conservation of energy: a law of physics that states that energy, itself, cannot be created and destroyed but can only alter its forms. For example, it is believed if one burned a piece of coal and collected all the smoke, ash and other particles which radiated from the burning and weighed them, one would have the same weight as before the coal was burned. Page 252.

conversation (with): close familiarity or acquaintance with something, as from constant use or study. Page 132.

convictions: mental states or conditions of being convinced; strong or firmly held beliefs. Page 296.

could not (cannot) but (be): could not (cannot) be, become or do anything else than what is mentioned; unable to prevent or avoid being. Page 12.

counsel, keep one's own: consult with oneself, advise oneself as to actions or matters of right and wrong. Page 138.

course (of something): 1. a systematic or orderly series of steps, as in *"The course of auditing."* Page 146.
2. the succession of stages through which something passes, as in *"the auditor must not be dismayed at the course of tone, but should simply persevere."* Page 146.

cousin: a person or thing related to another by similar natures, languages, geographical proximity, etc. Page 109.

crackling: exhibiting liveliness, vibrancy, etc. Literally, the making of slight cracking sounds rapidly repeated. Page 153.

Creative Processing: processing which has the preclear make, out of energy of his own creation, various forms, objects, distances and spaces—referred to as *mock-ups*. Creative Processing is fully described in Chapter Twenty-Three, Creative Processing. Page 58.

criminal-to-be: someone who will soon commit crimes. *To-be* is combined with other words to mean someone who will (soon) be what is being spoken of, such as bride-to-be. Page 127.

dams: is held back or confined as if by a *dam,* a barrier of earth, wall, etc., constructed across a stream to obstruct its flow or raise its level. Page 205.

Dante: Italian poet (1265–1321) who in his most important work, *The Divine Comedy,* describes his journey through Hell to Heaven. Inscribed above the entrance to Hell are the words: "Abandon all hope, ye who enter here." Page 123.

DC: abbreviation for *direct current,* electricity that flows in only one direction. Flashlight batteries and those used in most portable equipment are examples. Page 151.

debased: lowered in quality, value or character. Page 169.

DED: *DED* stands for *deserved action,* an incident the preclear does to another dynamic and for which he has no motivator—i.e., he punishes or hurts or wrecks something the like of which has never hurt him. Now he must justify the incident. He will use things which didn't happen to him. He claims that the object of his injury really deserved it, hence the word, which is a sarcasm. DED is described in *Scientology: A History of Man.* Page 302.

DEDEX: an incident which happens to a preclear *after* he has a DED. It is always on the same chain or subject, is always after the DED. It means the DED EXposed. It is covered guilt. Its effect on the preclear is all out of proportion to the actual injury to him. One would think he was murdered by the harsh word or the scratch. He will explain violently how terribly he has been used. DEDEX is described in *Scientology: A History of Man.* Page 302.

DED-DEDEX: auditing the preclear on DEDs and DEDEXes. Page 302.

deduction: the drawing of a conclusion by reasoning from data already known or assumed. Page 120.

degree that, to the: to the extent, amount, intensity, etc., that. Page 25.

despatch: a sending off to a destination or for a purpose. Page 285.

diabolical: extreme or exceedingly great in degree. Page 196.

diffident: lacking in self-confidence; reserved in manner. Page 164.

dimension: a measure of spatial extent, such as length, width or height. Page 91.

dirty words: words or phrases that are considered morally unclean or impure and offensive to accepted standards of decency. Page 295.

discernment: an act or instance of *discerning,* separating (a thing) mentally from another or others; recognizing as separate or different. Page 164.

discharging: a *discharge* is the flow of electricity which takes place between two oppositely charged objects when they touch together, or when a path is provided between the objects for electricity to flow. An example is the spark or jolt that you feel when you touch a doorknob after walking across a carpet on a dry day. A terminal is *discharging* against another terminal when the charge is allowed to flow from one to the other. Page 150.

discharging condenser: in an electronic circuit, a condenser can accumulate large quantities of energy and when releasing it produce a far greater effect than the electrical flow itself was capable of. *See* **condenser** and **discharging.** Page 150.

discovering to (someone): making possible the disclosure or revelation to someone of something covered up, hidden or previously unseen. Page 180.

dismayed: discouraged, disheartened or disappointed (by apparent danger or trouble). Page 146.

disparage: lower in rank or estimation; dishonor (by comparison with something inferior); undervalue. Page 137.

divergences: departures or deviations from a path, course, standard, pattern, etc. Page 165.

dossier: a complete file containing detailed information about a person. Page 130.

do what (one) will: used to mean that whatever one does, it doesn't matter because the condition or result will be the same. Page 149.

early Greek: pertaining to a writer, philosopher, etc., of Greece from around the third century B.C. to the first century B.C., a time of great cultural advancement. Page 131.

early-type: of, relating to or characteristic of a period of time near the beginning of a course of events. Specifically in this sense, relating to Dianetics auditing from 1950 to 1951, as in *"After a few hundred hours of early-type auditing."* Page 300.

edification: instruction or enlightenment; intellectual gain. Used ironically. Page 167.

effect that, to the: with the result or purpose of. Page 181.

Effort Processing: Effort Processing is done by running moments of physical stress. These are run either as simple efforts or counter-efforts, or as whole precise incidents. Such incidents as those which contain physical pain or heavy stress of motion (such as injuries, accidents or illnesses) are addressed by Effort Processing. Effort Processing is described in *Advanced Procedure and Axioms* and its companion lecture series *Thought, Emotion and Effort.* Page 302.

egress terminal: a means or place of going out; an exit. *Egress* means related to coming or going out. *Terminal* is where one starts or ends a journey. Page 195.

electric generators: machines or mechanical devices which produce electricity. Page 150.

Electropsychometric Auditing: the first operator's manual for the E-Meter, published in 1952. (*Electro* means electric or electricity, *psycho* means soul, and *meter* means measure.) Available in the *Technical Bulletins* volumes and the *Technique 88: Incidents on the Track Before Earth* lecture series package. Page 63.

emotional curve: that drop or rise on the Tone Scale attend to failure to control on any dynamic or to the recipient of an ally on any dynamic. The drop falls from above 2.5 down to Apathy, in a steep curve. It occurs in seconds or minutes or hours. The speed of its fall is an index of the severity of the failure. (*Attend* in this sense means associated with something or resulting or following from it.) Emotional curve is fully described in *Advanced Procedure and Axioms.* Page 302.

encompass: enclose mentally; comprehend. Also, to contain or include comprehensively. Page 53.

end in itself: a purpose or goal desired for its own sake (rather than to attain something else). Page 279.

End of Session Processing: refers to the series of processes at the end of *Self Analysis.* Page 212.

end, to this: for this purpose; for this reason. Page 160.

Entities, The: entities are fully described in *Scientology: A History of Man*. Page 160.

epistemology: a branch of philosophy that investigates the origin, nature, methods and limits of human knowledge. Page 122.

equanimity: stability or composure, especially under tension or strain; calmness. Page 169.

equates: is comparable to; is properly associated with; shows relationship such as equivalence between. Page 114.

equilibrium: a condition in which all acting influences and forces are opposed or cancelled by others, resulting in a stable, balanced or unchanging system. Page 15.

eschew: to avoid or keep away from (something harmful). Page 169.

exact: (as in *"exact science"*) characterized by strict adherence to standards or rules. Page 11.

Expanded GITA: *GITA* is short for *Give and Take Processing*. Expanded GITA is described in Standard Operating Procedure 8 in this book. Page 286.

facility: ability to do something with ease or skill. Page 168.

fair play: just and honorable treatment, action or conduct; respect for the rules, as in a game. Page 129.

fashion, in this: in the way or manner indicated. Page 109.

fashion, to: to make in a certain way; give a certain shape or form to. Page 17.

feeds back: returns or gives back to as the effect of some process such as the body giving a feeling, awareness or the like about a certain state or condition. Page 151.

field: a region, volume or space where a specific, measurable influence, force, etc., exists. Page 88.

Fifth Invader Force: reference to *invader forces,* an electronics people. The electronics people usually happen to be an evolutionary line which is on heavy gravity planets, and so they develop electronics. The reason you say invader forces at all is because at some time fairly early in their youth, they took off to conquer the whole MEST universe. Page 174.

fission bomb: an atomic bomb in which the center portion of an atom is split (fissioned) into smaller parts, accompanied by a significant release of energy. Page 3.

"V": same as Case V (five) or Step V. The definition of a (Case) V is "no mock-ups, only blackness." The term refers to the fifth step of Standard Operating Procedure wherein the auditor tests the preclear at each stage of the process to find a step the preclear can do and begins processing at that step. A preclear who had to be started at Step V of the process was called a "Case V." Page 202.

fixed (upon, to): caused to be placed on (to) something, as if by being firmly attached or fastened. Page 63.

fix on: to fasten, set or attach one's attention firmly on or upon something. Page 266.

flick: move or make something move with a quick sharp jerk. Page 93.

"flitter": there is this terrific cloud of gold sparks an individual will put out. That is making dimension points. Page 285.

flounders: struggles awkwardly, unsteadily or helplessly. Page 211.

focalize: adjust so as to come to a point or center where something becomes distinct and is in a state of clarity. Page 188.

follows out: pursues to a conclusion or final result. Page 254.

fore, to the: into a clearly visible place or position. Page 83.

form: the structure, shape or pattern of something as distinguished from the matter it is composed of. Page 252.

formulated: planned out in a definite, systematic and orderly fashion. Page 145.

forsakings: instances of abandoning, departing or withdrawing from. Page 108.

Freeing by Dichotomies: a process fully described in The Dichotomies. Page 160.

Freeing by Tone Scale: a process fully described in The Emotional Scale and Sub-zero Tone Scale. Page 160.

Freeing the Thetan by Concept and Feeling: a process that directs the preclear to "Get the concept that you need a body" and "Get the concept that you don't need the body." Page 160.

Freeing the Thetan by Orientation: a technique in which the auditor gets the preclear to pull himself out of the body. See Step II of Standard Operating Procedure, Issue 3 in this book. Page 160.

Freeing the Thetan by Positioning and Exhaustion of Flows: a technique in which the auditor takes the preclear outside his body and then blows the flows out. The auditor actually works him around his body by making him work against the flows. Page 160.

Freeing the Thetan by Present and Future: processing that emphasizes positive gain and the present and future rather than the negative gain of eradication of the past. Page 160.

fronted: faced in opposition; confronted. Page 57.

fronting: confronting, meeting someone or something as if face to face. Page 124.

Galaxy 13: the galaxy containing our solar system. A *galaxy* is a large system of stars held together by gravitation and isolated from similar systems by vast regions of space. Page 125.

gallantry: heroic bravery, especially in war or in a situation of great danger; nobility of spirit or action. Page 124.

garnish: to enhance (in appearance), to decorate; to make fancy or striking. Hence, by extension to equip for use. Page 253.

general semantics: a highly organized philosophical approach to language, developed by Alfred Korzybski (1879–1950). In the book, *Science and Sanity* (1933) Korzybski rejects Aristotle's belief that logic is two-valued (something is either A or B) and proposes an infinity-valued system. He further states that identification (as when Pavlov's dog identified the bell sound with food, causing a physiological reaction) is found in all known forms of mental ills. Page 82.

genesis: the coming into being of something; the initial stage of a developmental process; origin. Page 271.

geometry (of): the way the parts or elements of something are designed or arranged and fit together. Page 87.

Give and Take Processing: this process consists of causing the preclear to take in, in the order given, large numbers of things and, by bringing them into his body and condensing them and then sending them out, remedies excessive holding to articles, facsimiles, old sensation. The objects listed include vast numbers of the opposite sex; friends; bodies which might have been his own; hordes of parents and relations; many graves; an enormous number of buildings and homes, vast quantities of food; enormous quantities of raiment (clothing); vast sums of money in many forms, bills and coinage; great numbers of jewels; weapons and energy beams; communications; emotions; sensations. Give and Take Processing is contained in *The Factors* lecture series package supplement. Page 293.

given to: inclined to something or likely to do or be something; having a tendency, as in *"given to understand."* Page 116.

goes about: engages upon, deals with something. Page 254.

goes around: to often be in a particular state or behave in a particular way, as in *"That preclear who goes around believing he is other people is usually at the bottom end of the Tone Scale."* Page 117.

governing: exercising a determining influence; controlling or influencing. Page 303.

Governor, The: the speed of the preclear. How fast does he run, how fast he can change flows, how much energy he can make. It is an analogy to a *governor,* a mechanical device which controls the speed of an engine. It is used here to mean a sort of speed-control mechanism used by an individual to speed himself up or slow himself down in order to meet various situations in life. One can decide to run fast or slow and The Governor puts the theta facsimile of that speed into use, affecting the metabolism and everything else concerned with the body. To run slow it will pick up or postulate or imagine a slow facsimile and then run on it. Or it can postulate a fast theta facsimile and run on it. Further information can be found in the lecture of 24 October 1951, "Being Right." Available in the Research & Discovery volumes. Page 149.

gravitic: of or related to a force or feeling of attraction, as toward an object or point of influence, likened to *gravity,* the physical force by which bodies tend to move toward the center of the Earth. Page 266.

greater or lesser degree: used to emphasize that something is always the case, even though it is more true or noticeable in some situations than others. Page 105.

grosser: made up of material elements, thought of as lower in quality, level or value than something else (as contrasted with that which is spiritual). Page 17.

ground: to connect to the earth so that electrical charge will flow into the ground so that a harmless path is provided to drain off stray or excess electrical currents. Earth conducts electricity, so if an appliance, piece of equipment or any item that is electrically charged is connected to the ground, electrical energy will flow out of the item and into the earth. The human body also conducts electricity, and an electrical charge that is generated in the body will flow out of the body and into the earth if the body is in contact with it. Page 154.

grovel: humble oneself, perform an act of humiliation, as if lying face down before someone or something. Page 132.

harmonic(s): used to describe a frequency (number of vibrations per second) which is a multiple of a "fundamental" frequency. If one stretches a string or rubber band, and strikes it, a tone or note is produced. One can measure the number of times per second that string is vibrating. Another string, vibrating at certain, but different, multiples of that vibration rate will sound pleasing. This is calculated out mathematically such as 1, 1/2, 1/3, 1/4, etc. Such can be seen with strings in a piano, each one different in length and vibrating at different rates per second. By striking two or more at a time, simultaneously, one can hear which notes are harmonious (pleasing), when played together, and which are disharmonious (harsh or not pleasing). Thus, by extension, something which repeats characteristics at a higher or lower point on a scale will be harmonic and seem to be similar and agreeable. Page 38.

have to do with: are concerned or associated with. Page 219.

heavy: of great force, intensity, turbulence, etc., as in, *"severe pain or heavy emotional stress"* or *"He will find, occasionally, that he often has a difficult time when a particularly heavy facsimile is in restimulation."* Page 16.

hectic: characterized by a state of feverish excitement or activity; disturbing. Page 109.

heed: careful or close attention; notice; observation (usually with give or take). Page 291.

here and there: in this place and in that, at various times or places. Page 171.

Hindu: a native of India, who is a follower of the Indian religion of Hinduism, which emphasizes freedom from the material world through purification of desires and elimination of personal identity. Hindus believe that ultimate salvation is achieved from the endless cycle of birth to death when one merges or is absorbed into the "one divine reality" with all loss of individual existence. Page 220.

hitherto: until this time; up to the present time or the time in question. Page 17.

hovering: to remain floating, suspended or fluttering in the air. Hence, remaining (sometimes close at hand) in an uncertain, undecided state. Page 53.

humanities: the branches of learning concerned with human thought and relations, especially language, literature, history and philosophy, as distinguished from the sciences. Page 3.

hung up: halted or snagged. Page 311.

if anything: a phrase used to emphasize what has just been mentioned; perhaps even, as in *"Scientology is essentially a study of statics and kinetics. If anything, it is more exact than what are called the physical sciences."* Page 23.

imperishable: indestructible; enduring. Page 272.

implicitly: unquestioningly or unreservedly; absolutely. Page 285.

imponderable: something that cannot be precisely determined, measured or evaluated; not capable of being mentally weighed. Page 226.

indifferently: in a manner that is neither good nor bad in character or quality; average; routine. Page 192.

induction: the process of deriving general principles, theories, laws, etc., from particular facts or instances that have been observed. Page 273.

inferred: concluded something as probable on the basis of evidence and reasoning rather than from clear and detailed facts. Page 260.

infinite mind: the theory or belief that there is an absolute mind, the mind of the All, being present everywhere and independent of time and space; the source and foundation of existence, possessed of all possible power, wisdom and excellence, sometimes said in reference to God. Page 128.

infinity: that which is unable to be measured; the state or quality of being infinite, having no limit or end. Introduction.

in many directions: in regard to numerous areas or subjects; in many matters. Page 174.

in (one's) turn: one after the other, especially in a particular order. Page 31.

in point: that is relevant to the matter being considered; applicable, as in *"The case of the racing driver is in point."* Page 221.

in principle: theoretically. Used to mean that there is no reason something can't be done even though it may not yet have been carried out in detail. Page 186.

inroads: advances or penetrations, especially at the expense of something or someone. Page 18.

insentient: entirely without feeling, life or consciousness. Page 124.

insidious: operating or proceeding in an inconspicuous or seemingly harmless way but actually with grave effect; slowly and subtly harmful and destructive. Page 166.

in spite of: regardless of; without being affected by the particular factor mentioned. Page 83.

intent upon: determined to do, achieve or have something. Page 73.

interdependency: a state or condition of being unable to exist or survive without another or others. Page 13.

in the hands of: under the control, guidance or care of. Page 191.

in the light: with the help afforded by knowledge of (some fact, data, etc.). Page 84.

in this light: considered from a certain aspect; something which makes clearer or suggests a particular view of a subject. Page 195.

island universe: a distinct star system, such as that to which our Sun belongs, occupying a detached position in space. Page 124.

jocularly: jokingly; humorously or playfully. Page 117.

junior: subordinate to; smaller in scale to something larger or more powerful; of lesser importance. Page 124.

jurisprudence: the philosophy or science of law. Page 115.

key-out: cause something such as a mechanism in the mind to become deactivated. Literally, a *key* is a small manual device for opening, closing or switching electronic contacts. Hence, *key-out* means throw out of circuit so as to no longer be capable of causing an automatic reaction. Page 303.

kinetic: something that has considerable motion. Kinetics are further described throughout *Scientology 8-8008*. Page 15.

king in some corner: one that occupies and has total command and control over a certain designated area, sphere of activity, etc. *Corner* in this sense means any area or place. Hence, *"It was a poor man who was not king in some corner"* means a person is worthless or pitiful if he does not control or create in some specific sphere of knowledge, activity, interest or the like. Page 118.

Korzybski, Alfred: (1879–1950) Polish-American scholar who believed the imprecise use of language affected human behavior, causing confusion and miscommunication, misbehavior and even psychosomatic ills. In order to remedy this he employed various drills and conventions. For instance he employed the use of quotation marks around certain terms and numbered notations, such as placing the date beneath someone's name ($Smith_{1920}$ and $Smith_{1935}$), to prevent identification of people or things which were not in fact identical and thus distinguish in time when someone is being referred to. Page 82.

last shreds of, the: the very small quantities or fragments of something remaining after all others have gone, been done away with, etc. Page 130.

later numbered steps: reference to the case levels (steps) of Standard Operating Procedure, Issue 3. Consisting of seven processing steps, each step corresponds to a level of case, the later numbered steps being for cases not yet exteriorized. Page 171.

libido theory: a theory originated by the Austrian founder of psychoanalysis, Sigmund Freud (1856–1939), that the energy or urges motivating behavior are sexual in origin. *Libido* is Latin for desire or lust. Page 126.

line-charge: of or concerning a line charge, a whole group of incidents all together which themselves have a body of charge.

A *line charge* is simply a vast amount of relief coming off the case, sometimes accompanied by laughter. Page 109.

listless: having or showing little or no interest in anything; not caring, apathetic. Page 73.

lose no moment: waste no time. *Moment* is a minute portion of time. Page 192.

lot: something that befalls one because of or as if because of fortune or apparent fate; one's portion in life. Page 48.

low-combustion fuel: a reference to oxygen from the air and carbon from food which are mixed together and react in the human body producing heat and forming energy which is then used to carry out various functions including cell maintenance and growth, movement of the muscles, etc. *Low-combustion* means the chemical reaction between the substances (oxygen and carbon) is relatively slow and takes place at a low level, as opposed to high-combustion, as takes place in an automobile engine. Page 17.

macrocosm: a complex structure such as the world or the universe considered as a single entity that contains numerous (similar) smaller-scale structures and where the larger-scale structure is considered a representation or of similar structure to the smaller units. Example: The actions of his family unit reflected the social macrocosm in which he lived. The word *macro-* means enlarged, long or great. Page 259.

magnitude: (said of something physical or nonphysical) relative size, amount, extent, importance or influence. Page 71.

mark: set off as distinctive; distinguish, characterize. Page 72.

Mark: a particular make or model of equipment, frequently followed by a number designating the stage of development in design and construction, or the order of adoption. Mark I would be the first model. Mark 10,000 would be the 10,000th, allegedly a very advanced model. Page 167.

mastiff: a large, powerful dog with a large head, valuable as a watchdog. Page 118.

measured: adjusted to be suitable or effective. Page 101.

mechanical: concerned with or involving material objects or physical conditions or forces. Page 17.

member: a part of a human (or animal) body, especially a limb such as a leg or arm. Page 278.

microcosm: a little world; a thing regarded as representing in miniature the characteristics of something much larger. Page 259.

middle ground: a point halfway between extremes. Page 228.

middle years, in his: middle age, the time of human life between youth and old age, usually considered to be the years between 40 and 60. Page 73.

–8.0: the level of *Hiding* on the Sub-zero Tone Scale. Page 37.

mirth: joyfulness, gaiety or merriment, especially when characterized by laughter. Page 109.

mock-up: 1. a self-created image or object which exists as itself or symbolizes some object in the MEST universe; a mental image picture created by a thetan. Page 119.
2. make a mock-up of; make or create. Page 124.

modus operandi: a Latin term meaning mode of operation, way of operating or functioning. Page 251.

morrow, on the: the following or next day. Page 180.

mount up: increase by addition; to increase gradually in size and quantity. Page 174.

mystic: a person who claims to attain, or believes in the possibility of attaining, insight into mysteries that go beyond ordinary human knowledge, as by direct communication with the spiritual or divine. Page 205.

mysticism: the belief that it is possible to achieve knowledge of spiritual truths and God through contemplation or through deep and careful thought. Page 17.

mythical: relating or pertaining to an imaginary or fictitious thing or person. Page 174.

natural selection: the process by which forms of life having traits that better enable them to adapt to specific environmental pressures such as predators, changes in climate, competition for food or mates, will tend to survive and reproduce in greater numbers than others of their kind, thus ensuring the perpetuation of those favorable traits in succeeding generations. A *predator* is an animal that hunts, kills and eats other animals in order to survive, or any other organism that behaves in a similar manner. Page 17.

negative currents: in the phrase, *"positive and negative currents,"* flows (currents) of very, very small particles which have either positive or negative charges. *Positive currents* are currents of positively charged particles flowing through a substance, such as through the liquid in a car battery. *Negative currents* are currents of negatively charged particles flowing through a substance, such as through copper wire. Small particles can either be positively charged or negatively charged or neutral. When charged, particles are attracted to their opposite charge and repel their like charge and hence flow. Page 39.

Negative Exteriorization: a procedure to exteriorize someone: "Try *not* to be a foot behind your head." You tell him not to get out of his head. Page 302.

Nietzsche, Friedrich: Friedrich Wilhelm Nietzsche (1844–1900), German philosopher and poet. In his book *Thus Spake Zarathustra,* Nietzsche denounced all religion and the traditional religious values of the masses, whom he termed the "herd," and promoted the "morals of masters," a doctrine of perfecting a "superman" who is liberated from all values. His philosophy is regarded as having influenced the attitudes of the Nazi regime in Germany. Zarathustra (or Zoroaster) was the name of a Persian prophet in the sixth century B.C. Page 228.

Nirvana: the goal of the Hindus. Hindu beliefs are that "Reality is One" (Brahma) and that ultimate salvation, and release from the endless cycle of birth to death is achieved when one merges or is absorbed into the "one divine reality" with all loss of individual existence. Page 48.

node: as used in this book, it refers to the crest (topmost part) of the wave. *Node* in this sense is a thing that projects or extends outwards or upwards. *See also* **wavelength.** Page 32.

noise wave: a complex wave with a random, irregular pattern. Page 31.

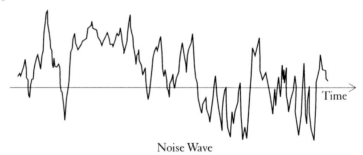

Noise Wave

nothing if not: used to emphasize a particular quality that something has; above everything; undoubtedly. Page 114.

older gods: the thetans who built this universe. Page 118.

"on the same wavelength": in sympathy or rapport. Page 168.

order of magnitude: the relative size, extent or degree of influence, power or the like. *Order* is any class, kind or sort, as of persons or things, distinguished from others by nature or character. *Magnitude* is quantity or greatness of size, extent, importance or influence. Page 128.

outthrust: to extend or cause to extend outward; (forcibly) push outwards. Page 238.

overreached: surpassed in terms of ability, control, etc. Page 192.

paradoxes: people, situations, acts, etc., that seem to have contradictory or inconsistent qualities. Page 253.

paramount: greatest in importance or significance. Page 171.

party: a person (amongst others) that participates or is involved in some action, situation, etc. Page 202.

passes for: is accepted as or believed to be. Often used with the implication of actually being something else. Page 120.

pawn: literally, one of the pieces of smallest size and value in the game of chess. Hence, a thing which is used or manipulated to further another's purposes. Page 196.

Pekingese: a small pet dog of a Chinese breed with a short, flat nose, a long, straight, silky coat and a tail that curls over its back. Page 118.

physical sciences: any of the sciences, such as physics and chemistry, that study and analyze the nature and properties of energy and nonliving matter. Page 23.

physicist: a scientist who specializes in *physics,* the science that deals with matter, energy, motion and force, including what these things are, why they behave as they do and the relationship between them, as contrasted to the life sciences such as biology, which studies and observes living organisms such as animals and plants. Page 3.

plateau: a point or stage reached after a period of development or progress. Page i.

played (against): literally, aimed or directed, sometimes continuously. Used figuratively. Page 151.

player: a player of a game. *"Below the level of 'player'"* refers to the scale of games whose component parts are: maker of games, players, assistant players, pieces and broken pieces. Games are described in the LRH lectures of 12 December 1952, "Game Processing" and "Games/Goals" in the lecture series *The Philadelphia Doctorate Course Lectures.* Page 196.

pockmarked: marked or scarred as though with *pockmarks,* small pits or scars on the surface of something. Used figuratively. Page 3.

portals: doorways, gates or entrances, especially large and imposing ones. Page 123.

posed: put forward; presented. Page 14.

positive currents: in the phrase, *"positive and negative currents,"* flows (currents) of very, very small particles which have either positive or negative charges. *Positive currents* are currents of positively charged particles flowing through a substance, such as through the liquid in a car battery. *Negative currents* are currents of negatively charged particles flowing through a substance, such as through copper wire. Small particles can either be positively charged or negatively charged or neutral. When charged, particles are attracted to their opposite charge and repel their like charge and hence flow. Page 39.

predicated (on): (said of a statement or action) based or established on. Page 308.

---

predominates: is most common; greatest in number or amount. Page 153.

preeminent: superior to or notable above all others; outstanding. Introduction.

pretext: something that is put forward to conceal a true purpose or object; excuse. Page 130.

process, in the: in the course of or while something else is occurring. Page 300.

profitable: of use, benefit or advantage. Page 93.

promulgation: the act of making something widely known; the setting forth or teaching of something publicly. Page 119.

proof: 1. a sequence of steps, statements or demonstrations that leads to a valid conclusion. Page 24.
2. fully successful in resisting or withstanding (something or someone). Page 195.

quasi-: seeming; having a likeness to something; resembling. Page 292.

Randomity: a process dealing with randomity. For example: "What have you selected for your randomity in present time?" "What has selected you for its randomity in present time?" "What have others selected for randomity from others in present time?" Page 160.

ransacking: hunting thoroughly and searchingly through something in a rough, forceful way. Used figuratively. Page 122.

ratio: the corresponding relationship between two or more things; proportional relation. A *ratio* is sometimes expressed as a number or amount in relationship to another number or amount. For example, if a person spends ten hours inside and one hour outside, the ratio is 10:1 or ten to one. Page 25.

reaction time: the amount of time it takes someone to react to or do something in the environment (or during a test), such as making a decision, solving a problem, etc. Page 163.

recant: retract, renounce or disavow a former opinion or belief; especially to make a formal or public confession of error. Page 205.

reclamation: a restoration as to productivity, usefulness or morality. Page 127.

revulse: withdraw; strongly pull back or away. Page 179.

revulsion: a (strong) pulling or drawing back or away. Page 39.

"rich man may as well try to get into Heaven, as a camel through the eye of a needle, a": from a story in the Bible of a rich man who, when told eternal life could be his if he sold everything he had and gave it to the poor, rejected the offer and went sadly away. Whereupon it was said, "It is easier for a camel to go through the eye of a needle than for a rich man to enter the kingdom of God!" Page 115.

rickety: liable to fall or break down because of being weak; shaky. Page 151.

rising scale: in Rising Scale Processing, a reference to the action of the preclear changing or shifting his postulates upward toward a higher level on the Chart of Attitudes. Rising Scale Processing is fully described in Chapter Twenty-Four, Postulate Processing. Page 113.

ritual: any established procedure, pattern, routine or agreement. Page 285.

rock: a source of danger or destruction, suggestive of a shipwreck. Page 124.

run (a) course: complete its natural development without interference. *Course* in this sense means the continuous passage or progress through a succession of stages. Page 226.

Running Engrams: a method of Standard Operating Procedure 1950 or 1951. It is a method of making the individual re-assume control of a period where he has abandoned control of space, energy and objects. You make him re-assume control by going through it again and running through it again and demonstrating to him that he had a better control of it than he supposed. Page 160.

Running Live Flow: running a live flow. That is running present time flow. You just manufacture energy and blow things up with it. Page 160.

Running Locks: (Lock Scanning) a process which starts the preclear from a point in the past, with which he has made solid contact, up through all similar incidents, without verbalization. This is done over and over, each time trying to start at an earlier incident of the same kind, until the preclear extroverts on the subject of the chain. Lock Scanning is a standardized drill, started on signal and ended with the preclear saying he is again in present time. Page 160.

Running Ridges (Circuits): the running of ridges as such, because that is the running of circuits. You blow a ridge by making it flow or putting direct energy at it. When the thetan is outside the body, he can actually reach into the body with a beam and blow the ridges up that are all through the brain, all through the spine, anyplace in the body where the nerves are pinched or anything, he can straighten out the residual energy. Ridge Running is also covered in Step IV of Standard Operating Procedure, Issue 3 in this book. Page 160.

Running Secondaries: running grief charges, the subject of loss. Run the same way one runs an engram. Start them in at the beginning and they can be in terror, be in fear, be any of those things—just tell the preclear to start in and he runs it on through. Page 160.

saddled: burdened or loaded (with). Page 188.

sake of, for the: for the purpose or end of. Page 179.

sanitaria: institutions for the mentally ill. Page 107.

Schopenhauer: Arthur Schopenhauer (1788–1860), German philosopher who believed that the will to live is the fundamental reality and that this will, being a constant striving, cannot be satisfied and only causes suffering. Page 57.

science: knowledge; comprehension or understanding of facts or principles, classified and made available in work, life or the search for truth. A science is a connected body of demonstrated truths or observed facts systematically organized and bound together under general laws. It includes trustworthy methods for the discovery of new truth within its domain and denotes the application of scientific methods in fields of study previously considered open only to theories based on subjective, historical or undemonstrable, abstract criteria. The word *science,* when applied to Scientology, is used in this sense—the most fundamental meaning and tradition of the word—and not in the sense of the *physical* or *material* sciences. Page 3.

self-aggrandizement: the ambitious or ruthless pursuit of increased personal importance, wealth, reputation or power. Page 131.

Self Analysis in Scientology: a converted edition of the original *Self Analysis* to include Creative Processing. Page 212.

semantics: of or relating to meaning, especially meaning in language; the meaning of a word, phrase, sentence or text. Page 192.

semantics, general: a highly organized philosophical approach to language, developed by Alfred Korzybski (1879–1950). In the book, *Science and Sanity* (1933) Korzybski rejects Aristotle's belief that logic is two-valued (something is either A or B) and proposes an infinity-valued system. He further states that identification (as when Pavlov's dog identified the bell sound with food, causing a physiological reaction) is found in all known forms of mental ills. Page 82.

servomechanism: a mechanism that serves, services or aids something. Specifically, *"The human mind is a servomechanism to all mathematics"* because mathematics is something which Man uses to solve problems: without the human mind mathematics is of no use. Page 84.

set back: delayed or hindered in progress. Page 165.

set in: (of something unpleasant or unwelcome) begin and seem likely to continue as if situated or fixed in a specified place or position. Page 121.

shalt, thou: *thou shalt* is an archaic form of *you shall,* used in formal writing such as in the Bible. Page 166.

sharply: attentively; with close and keen observation. Page 73.

shorthand: a short and simple way of expressing or representing something. Page 84.

shotgun: covering a wide area or field. A shotgun fires many small particles (shot) that spread out to cover a wider area. Page 307.

shuns: a humorous use of the word *shuns* with a double meaning. It refers to terms ending in "-tion," specifically invalida*tion,* and evalua*tion*. The word ending "-tion" is pronounced "shun" in English and is added to the end of words to form nouns. It also refers to the word *shun* which means something that must be avoided or kept away from, as being undesirable. Page 169.

shy away: draw back or avoid. Page 166.

sine wave: a type of simple wave that has regular smooth vibrations at regular intervals. Page 31.

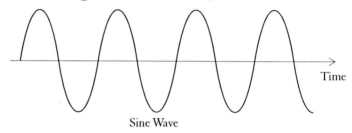

Time

Sine Wave

singular: of unusual quality, remarkably good, exceptional; unique. Page 220.

situation: manner of being situated; location or position with reference to environment. Page 23.

slaying of a roaring beast of fire: a reference to doing battle with and killing a dragon, a legendary monster in the folklore of many European and Asian cultures. Legends describe dragons as huge, lizardlike, winged creatures that breathe fire and have a long, scaly tail and often guard a sought-after treasure. Slaying such a beast was considered a difficult and awe-inspiring feat. Page 124.

snake pits: intensely chaotic or disagreeable places or situations. In primitive cultures, literally large pits containing poisonous snakes into which victims were thrown for execution or as a test of endurance. Page 122.

snare: a kind of trap for small animals, usually consisting of a noose which jerks tight upon the release of a spring trigger.

Hence, anything that tempts or attracts and by which a person is entangled or trapped unexpectedly. Page 127.

sober: based on facts and rational thinking rather than on speculation. Page 17.

SOP: abbreviation for *Standard Operating Procedure.* Page 201.

sordid: characteristic of depressing, degraded drudgery or dullness. Page 122.

sound: marked by solidity, firmness or stability; unshakable. Also, free from errors or defects. Page 160.

Spacation: *Spacation* is described in Step III of Standard Operating Procedure 8 in this book. Page 286.

space warps: imaginary distortions of space-time that enable phenomena to occur which are contrary to the accepted laws of nature or the physical universe. Page 185.

spasm: a sudden (involuntary) muscular contraction or a sudden grasping movement; used figuratively. Page 130.

spectrum: a continuous range or entire extent of something between two extreme or opposite points. Page 23.

speculation: a conclusion, an opinion, or a theory reached by guessing due to incomplete information or evidence. Page 241.

spin: go into a state of mental confusion, likened to spinning or rotating around. Page 300.

spirit: the attitude or intentions with which someone undertakes or regards something; inclination or a tendency of a specified kind. Page 129.

spiritualism: the doctrine or belief that the spirits of the dead can and do communicate with the living, especially through a person (a medium). Page 17.

Standard Operating Procedure: a series of seven auditing steps issued in November 1952. Often abbreviated SOP, it was the first in the sequence of processes such as SOP 3, SOP 5 and SOP 8 which contained the technology of how to make a Theta Clear. SOP 3 can be found in this book in Standard Operating Procedure, Issue 3 and SOP 8 can be found in this book in Standard Operating Procedure 8. Page 18.

Standard Operating Procedure 8: a technique developed after careful observation of preceding operating procedures and their degree of workability in auditors' hands. SOP 8 emphasizes *positive gain* and the present and future rather than *negative gain* of eradication of the past. LRH called this Standard Operating Procedure 8 to signify its importance and designate it with the number 8 to ensure it would go in company with 8-8008. Page 291.

Standard Operating Procedure, Issue 3: a technique consisting of seven processing steps. The number 3 was assigned to this procedure as it was the third revision of the original Standard Operating Procedure. It was the current version when *Scientology 8-8008* was originally published and is the version that directly corresponds with the start of the Philadelphia Doctorate Course. A glossary of terms written by LRH for Standard Operating Procedure appears in this book in Standard Operating Procedure, Issue 3. Page 170.

standby: something that can always be relied on, is effective and therefore a favorite or frequent choice. Page 254.

standpoint: a position from which things (such as objects, principles or the like) are or may be viewed and according to which they are compared and judged, as in *"From the standpoint of the* MEST *universe."* Page 41.

static: something with no motion, no particle and no wavelength. Statics are further described throughout *Scientology 8-8008*. Page 15.

step away from: withdraw from (something) so as to be no longer influenced by it, as if by taking a single short movement with the foot. Page 124.

straits: a position of difficulty, distress or need. Page 298.

sub-divided: divided into units that are smaller still. Page 14.

sub-divisible: can have its divided parts divided into units that are smaller still. Page 18.

subject (to): that can be affected or influenced or controlled by a particular thing. Page 97.

sublime: belonging to the highest regions of thought, activity, beingness, etc. Page 131.

subservient: acting in a subordinate capacity, in compliance and obedience to. Page 253.

such an extent, to: used to show how great an effect something has; so much that. Page 115.

summed: brought into or contained in a brief and comprehensive statement; summarized. Page 52.

supine: at effect, failing to act; inactive. From the original meaning, lying on one's back with the face or front upward. Page 121.

surcease: a bringing or coming to an end; a stopping. Page 131.

susceptible: of such a nature, character or constitution as to be capable of submitting to an action, process or operation; capable of being influenced or affected by. Page 272.

sway: controlling influence; rule; dominion; power. Page 260.

swing: move in a curve, as around a central point, as in *"wherever suns shine and planets swing."* Page 131.

take effect: go into operation; produce a result (as expected or intended). Page 182.

take on: acquire or display something, such as a form, appearance, etc. Page 246.

tendered: offered formally in writing; offered freely as for acceptance. Page 241.

tenement: run-down and often overcrowded apartment house. Page 225.

terminal, egress: a means or place of going out; an exit. *Egress* means related to coming or going out. *Terminal* is where one starts or ends a journey. Page 195.

terms: periods or lengths of time normally thought of as having limits, as in *"He may find a very young person is still in terms of growth."* Page 73.

Theta Clear: a being who is reasonably stable outside the body and does not come back into the body simply because the body is hurt. No other condition is necessary. Page 107.

Thetan, The: refers to the processing of the thetan. As covered in this book, *"With Creative Processing, Postulate Processing is the primary and highest method of processing a thetan and it constitutes Scientology 8-8008."* Page 160.

thine: archaic term for *your,* normally used in formal writing such as in the Bible. Page 166.

This Is Scientology: a work originally written for the June 1953 issue of the *Journal of Scientology. This Is Scientology* is published in *The Creation of Human Ability.* Page 304.

this way and that: indicating various directions of motion or relative position as distinct from one another; in a variety of angles or aspects (from which a thing can be presented to view). Page 171.

thou: archaic form of the word *you,* normally used in formal writing such as in the Bible. Page 166.

tie-up(s): literally, to fasten (a thing) with a cord or band tied around it, so as to prevent it from moving or falling apart; hence a binding, restraining or confining of something or someone; a hindering from acting or being free. Page 169.

to the effect that: with the result or purpose of. Page 181.

tracement: a locating or discovering by searching or researching evidence, often with the idea of following down something or going backwards from its latest or most evident existence. Page 196.

traded upon: taken advantage of, especially selfishly or unfairly; made use of for one's own ends. Page 121.

transient: lasting only a short time; existing briefly; temporary. Page 272.

travail: pain or suffering resulting from physical struggle or mental conflict. Page 123.

turned on and off: made to start operating (turned on) and to stop operating (turned off) as if by means of a switch or button. Page 92.

under the hands of: subject to the power, control, influence or direction of. *Hands* in this sense means, possession or power; control or custody. Page 120.

ungoverned: out of control; unregulated. Page 82.

unit: something regarded as an independent whole and incapable of being divided or separated. Page 18.

unthwarted: unopposed in the successful attainment or fulfillment of a desire, purpose or goal; unfrustrated; undefeated. Page 260.

unto: a formal way of saying *to,* showing that something is given to someone. Page 41.

"V": same as Case V (five) or Step V. The definition of a (Case) V is "no mock-ups, only blackness." The term refers to the fifth step of Standard Operating Procedure wherein the auditor tests the preclear at each stage of the process to find a step the preclear can do and begins processing at that step. A preclear who had to be started at Step V of the process was called a "Case V." Page 202.

vested interest: a special interest in protecting or promoting that which is to one's own personal advantage. *Vested interests* are those who seek to maintain or control an existing activity, arrangement or condition from which they derive private benefit. Page 192.

vital: endowed with, or possessed of, life; animate; having remarkable energy. Page 83.

war cry: a cry, word, phrase, etc., shouted in charging or in rallying to attack; battle cry. By extension, a slogan, phrase or motto used to unite a political party, gather support for a cause, etc. Page 194.

watershed: having to do with events or occurrences of crucial importance; decisive; key. Literally, an area or ridge of land that separates waters flowing to different rivers, seas, etc. *Shed* here is used in the sense of ridge of high ground. Page ii.

wavelength: wavelength is the relative distance from node (crest) to node (crest) in any flow of energy. In the MEST universe, wavelength is commonly measured by centimeters or meters. The larger the number, the lower the wavelength is considered to be on the gradient scale of wavelengths. The smaller the number, the higher the wavelength is considered to be on the gradient scale. *See also* **node.** Page 15.

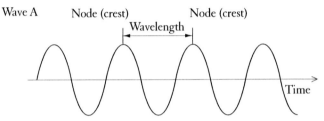

The smaller the distance between crests of the wave, the higher the wavelength is considered to be on the gradient scale of wavelengths.

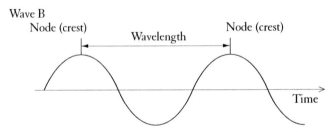

The larger the distance between crests of the wave, the lower the wavelength is considered to be on the gradient scale of wavelengths.

weighty(ier): serious and having much importance; of great consequence or significance. Page 53.

will: the faculty of conscious and especially of deliberate action; the power of control one has over his own actions; the act or process of using one's choice. Page 57.

willy-nilly: whether one likes or desires it or not. Page 265.

win through: to survive difficulties and reach a desired or satisfactory end. Page 123.

withered: caused something to become weak or to lose its strength or force. Page 122.

woof and warp: variation of *warp and woof,* the basic material or foundation of a structure, entity, etc.; a reference to the threads that make up a woven fabric: the *warp* threads run lengthwise on the loom (an apparatus for making fabric) and the *woof* threads run crosswise. Page 81.

yet, is: still; in spite of that; however. Page 15.

$\mathcal{I}$NDEX

A

A=A=A=A, 81

aberrated

preclears, "solid" to the degree that they are, 25

aberration, 47

body and, 226

Code of Honor and, 137

confused universes and, 251

genetic entity and, 193

inability to create and, 226

logic and, 273

postulates and, 179

scarcity of things, 265

single source of, 29

test of, 284

uncertainty and, 203

aberrative incidents

reversal of havingness, 53

ability

make the able more able, 12

surrendering of, 120

absolutes

symbolized by mathematics, 84

unobtainable, 14, 84, 163

abundance

Expanded GITA and, 294

AC, 151

see also **alternating current**

Acceptance–Rejection, 152

accident-prone, 114

accidents, 311

action, 33

bad, definition, 225

conditions necessary to, 30

cycle of havingness and, 71

definition, 51

energy and, 51

good, definition, 225

ideas senior to, 58

right versus wrong, 14

Tone Scale, 144

actuality

versus reality, 252

adhesion, 39

ruler of the universe, 129

treats words and thoughts as objects, 25

use lightest possible methods, 298

Punishing other bodies, 144

punishment

MEST universe and, 129

Q

qualities of energy, 31

R

racing driver, 221

Randomity

processing, 160

randomity

responsibility and, 105

rationalization, 272

Reach and Withdraw, 310, 311

preclear not responding to, 311

reactive (memory) banks, 17

contain, 16

reactive mind

definition, 207

description, 18

reduction of the command value of, 19

reactive thought

definition, 57

reality, 40–42

agreement, 283

consideration of particles, 284

definition, 41, 203

delusion, 167

established by, 40

lack of motion, 40

never compromise, 138

of universes, 252

own universe and, 42

versus actuality, 252

Reality–Unreality, 121

reason

dichotomy, 152

regret, 138

of competence, 132

related experiences

description, 77

relationships

table of, 77

responsibility, 105–109, 167

communication and, 285

dichotomy, 152

for his own created illusions, 206

gradient scale of, 105

level, 105

perception and, 40

∞